THEY LIVED IN THE WHITE HOUSE

BY THE AUTHOR OF

We Came to America

Two Loves for Jenny Lind

Holiday Round Up (with Lucile Pannell)

THEY LIVED
in the
WHITE HOUSE

By Frances Cavanah

with illustrations by Clifford Schule

MACRAE SMITH COMPANY: PHILADELPHIA

Library of Congress Catalog Card Number 59-13259
Manufactured in the United States of America

5910

ACKNOWLEDGMENTS

The author and editor wishes to express her appreciation to the following for permission to quote from copyrighted material:

Dodd, Mead & Company, *for quotation from* RECOLLECTIONS OF FULL YEARS *by Helen Herron Taft. Reprinted by permission of Dodd, Mead & Company.*

Doubleday & Company, Inc., *for quotation from* WHITE HOUSE DIARY *by Henrietta Nesbitt. Copyright, 1948, by Henrietta Nesbitt. Reprinted by permission of Doubleday & Co., Inc.*

Harper & Brothers, *for quotations from* THIS I REMEMBER *by Eleanor Roosevelt; for quotations from* MEMORIES OF THE WHITE HOUSE *and* THROUGH FIVE ADMINISTRATIONS, *by Colonel W. R. Crook; for an excerpt from* IN THE DAYS OF MY FATHER *by Jesse R. Grant. Copyright, 1925, by Harper & Brothers. Copyright, 1953, by Nell Grant Cronan and Chapman Grant. The excerpt from the letter written by Mark Twain to Ruth Cleveland is from* GROVER CLEVELAND, THE MAN AND THE STATESMAN, *by Robert McElroy, published, 1923, by Harper & Brothers.*

Houghton Mifflin Company, *for quotations from* FORTY-TWO YEARS IN THE WHITE HOUSE *by Irwin Hood (Ike) Hoover. Copyright, 1934, by James Osborne Hoover and Mildred Hoover Stewart. Reprinted by permission of Houghton Mifflin Company.*

Eleanor Wilson McAdoo, *for quotations from* THE WOODROW WILSONS. *Copyright, 1937.*

The Macmillan Company, *for quotation from* THE ROOSEVELT FAMILY OF SAGAMORE HILL *by Hermann Hagedorn, copyright, 1954. Used with the permission of The Macmillan Company.*

Fleming H. Revell Company *for excerpts from* THE WHITE HOUSE GANG *by Earle Looker. Reprinted by permission of Fleming H. Revell Company.*

United Feature Syndicate, Inc. *for quotation from "My Day," syndicated column by Eleanor Roosevelt. Reprinted by permission of the United States Feature Syndicate, Inc.*

J. Frank West, *for excerpt from* TAD LINCOLN'S FATHER, *by Julie Taft Bayne, his grandmother.*

THIS BOOK IS DEDICATED TO MY NIECE
Marjorie C. Cavanah

Preface

The American people have always shown a warm and friendly interest in the families of our Presidents; and they are proud of the big, white-pillared mansion at 1600 Pennsylvania Avenue where all of our Presidents except George Washington have lived. They feel that it is *their* White House, because it belongs —not only to the family that occupies it for a few years—but to every American citizen. Thousands of sightseers who pass along the wide corridors are reminded of the history that has been made there. But the White House is also a home, and they feel a natural curiosity about the family life that goes on upstairs. Usually they are even more interested, if there are teenagers dancing in the East Room or youngsters romping over the wide lawns. In a sense these boys and girls are the sons and daughters of the nation, and the American people regard them with affection.

Being President of the United States is one of the hardest jobs in the world. He must constantly make decisions, sometimes affecting millions of people. His task is harder because he lives in a spotlight, and occasionally he tries to escape into a private life of his own. From the time of George Washington, most of our Presidents—who are very much like other fathers and grandfathers—have found the relaxation they needed with the younger members of their families. Abraham Lincoln's burden did not seem quite so heavy because Tad was there. During the darkest days of World War II, Franklin D. Roosevelt had thirteen adoring grandchildren who trooped in and out of the big rooms. Dwight D. Eisenhower delights in the company of four grandchildren who—to quote his daughter-in-law—are "just like other kids."

In the following chapters some of the boys and girls who lived in the White House speak for themselves, and you may read of their experiences in their own words. Parents, friends, and members of the White House staff are frequently quoted, and quotations from old newspapers help to tell the story. The purpose of this book is to show these White House young people as they appeared in their own time, and to those who knew them best. Nelly Custis is included, although the mansion in which George Washington, her step-grandfather, was so interested, was not completed in time for him to live there. Nelly undoubtedly knew about the plans and shared his enthusiasm during the days it was being built.

The search for firsthand material led to books written by those who have known the different Presidential families; to family letters and scrapbooks and to newspaper files. Sometimes an account was shortened or adapted to meet the needs of modern young readers, but the meaning and style of the original were carefully preserved. Chapters written entirely by the author, together with such descriptive details as were necessarily added, were based on contemporary accounts. Actual conversations were quoted, sometimes in shortened form. In occasional instances, when dialogue had to be imagined, the conversations might logically have taken place.

Correspondence or personal interviews with men and women who once lived in the White House or with their descendants were also sources of information and inspiration. Margaret Johnson Patterson Bartlett reported some of the stories which her father, Andrew Johnson Patterson, told her of the days when he lived in the White House with his grandfather, Andrew Johnson. Marion Cleveland Amen permitted me to read some of the unpublished letters of her mother, Mrs. Grover Cleveland. Marthena Harrison Williams shared her memories of her visits with her grandfather, Benjamin Harrison. Charles Taft, son of William Howard Taft, talked of his boyhood experiences. I wish to thank them and also Dean Francis B. Sayre of the National Cathedral in Washington who gave me a personal interview. This grandson of Woodrow Wilson was the last baby to be born in the White House.

The author is grateful to Anna Roosevelt Halsted and others for their gracious letters. Watt P. Marchman, Director of the Rutherford B. Hayes Library, Fremont, Ohio, kindly furnished me with copies of newspaper references to the children of Rutherford B. Hayes, culled from the extensive collection of Hayes scrapbooks in the library. Among others who have been helpful are Eugene E. Patton, author and former State Senator in Tennessee; Pauline Bonney, who lent me her scrapbooks of Washington, D.C. newspaper clippings; and Olive Seltzer who prepared the manuscript for the printer. The Washingtoniana Collection of the District of Columbia Public Library was a source of much interesting information. Most of my research was done in the Library of Congress and I am especially grateful to the librarians in the Manuscript Division and the Newspaper Periodical Room. I also wish to thank Arnold C. Tovell, editor of the Macrae Smith Company, whose understanding of each problem that arose and many excellent suggestions helped to make this book possible.

FRANCES CAVANAH
Washington, D.C.

Contents

contents continued

THEY LIVED IN THE WHITE HOUSE

1 ❧ Our First President and Nelly Custis

Nelly Custis, holding tight to General Washington's hand, left the house at number 10 Cherry Street. Tut, her eight-year-old brother, was already seated beside his grandmother in the coach waiting at the door. A crowd had gathered to watch the President's family start on their afternoon drive.

"Hurrah for His Excellency," someone cried. "Hurrah for Mistress Washington!" A boy about ten, Nelly's own age, gave a shout, "Hurrah for Nelly Custis."

Nelly blushed as she took her seat in the handsome carriage. Usually the cheers were all for George Washington. He was the first man to be elected President and was now living in New York, the new nation's temporary capital. The four cream-colored horses pawed the cobblestones, impatient to be off.

"Oh, Grandpa!" Nelly sank back against the cushions with a contented sigh.

Her brother, George Washington Parke Custis, who sat facing her, grinned as the beautiful horses trotted down the street.

Both Tut, as his grandmother called him, and Nelly missed Mt. Vernon, their home in Virginia. There were times when they felt a little lonely, but they loved their grandparents very much. All four of them looked forward to their afternoon drive together.

"Nelly! Tut! I have news for you," said Martha Washington. "Your tutor will be ready to begin your lessons again tomorrow."

"Yes, Grandmamma," Nelly replied, in a small voice. Tut swallowed hard. They had studied with a tutor, or teacher, at home. Now that they had come to New York, perhaps they had hoped to forget about lessons for a while.

They soon learned that they had the same old duties to perform. A part of every morning was spent with their tutor. Afterwards Nelly sat with her grandmother, learning to embroider. Then it was time to practice on her harpsichord, an instrument somewhat like a piano. The President had paid a thousand dollars for that harpsichord, and Mistress Washington had copied most of her music by hand. Although Nelly tried to feel grateful, sometimes she could not keep from crying. Doing finger exercises was very dull.

One-two! One! two! She went over them again and again, as the tears poured down her cheeks.

One day she slipped into the soft strains of a minuet, but her eyes kept wandering toward the window. Outside the green lawn sloped gently toward the East River, and she yearned to run outside and watch the boats. New York Bay seemed filled with boats; they plied endlessly back and forth. Nelly's hands, resting on the keyboard, forgot to play the familiar tune.

"Child, what are you thinking of?" Mistress Washington spoke sharply, as she looked up from her sewing. "Not of the Mozart minuet, I feel sure."

Nelly's cheeks were a bright pink as she bent over her music, and there was no more daydreaming. At last the clock struck two. No more practice for that day! She hurried up the carved staircase to her room. Here she brushed her soft brown curls and put on her prettiest dimity frock. By the time she joined the family in the dining room for their midafternoon dinner, she was her old laughing self again.

The President smiled at her fondly. He liked to hear her gay chatter. She was a good mimic, and her clever imitations of some of the pompous people who came to see him could always make him chuckle.

Many people wanted to see the President, and the Cherry Street house always seemed crowded. After a few months he decided to move into a bigger house on Broadway. The new home was much nearer Federal Hall, where Congress was meeting and trying to decide an important question: where should the permanent capital be located? For weeks the members argued. At last they voted to build an entirely new city near the Potomac River. The President was pleased. Congress asked him to choose the exact site, and he selected a wooded area twelve miles up the river from his beloved Mt. Vernon.

"The city of Washington in the territory of Columbia!" This was the official name on which Congress had decided, and Nelly liked the sound of the words. But her grandfather was modest. He always called it "the Federal City."

He knew, and Congress knew, that building a new city would take time, and it was decided to move the capital to Philadelphia for the next ten years. Nelly was not quite twelve when the Washington family moved into the comfortable mansion owned by Robert Morris, the Philadelphia patriot.

From then on her grandfather was even busier than before. Pierre L'Enfant, an army engineer who had come from France to fight in the American Revolution, was asked to draw up the plans for the future capital. He and the President often met in a house in the village of Georgetown near the site of the new city. Sometimes Thomas Jefferson, the Secretary of State, joined them, and they talked far into the night. They wanted to make the capital of the United States the most beautiful in the world. Again and again during the next six years, the President visited his Federal City. There was much to be done, and the work went slowly.

Meanwhile, in Philadelphia, the Custis children were growing up. Tut went away to school. Nelly, at sixteen, was a charming young woman. "Her sweetness equals her beauty, and that is perfect," said one foreign visitor.

Nelly's friends were often invited to the presidential mansion. Occasionally, the President would slip away from his desk and go into the drawing room, where they were playing some game or dancing the Virginia reel. He liked to watch them but suddenly the room would become very quiet. No one was laughing. No one was talking, and he realized this was because Nellie's friends stood in such awe of him. Sadly, the great George Washington would turn away and close the door behind him. He did not want to spoil their fun.

Although Nelly's grandfather was such an important man, she knew him too well and loved him too much ever to feel afraid of him. She looked forward to Sunday, which he usually spent with his family. She would play for him on the harpsichord and sing his favorite songs. He would talk about the Federal City.

It is easy to imagine him seated at a table, with a map spread out before him, while Nelly peered over his shoulder. Although Monsieur L'Enfant was no longer in charge, many of his plans were being carried out. Grandpapa's map showed where future streets would be cut through the forests. Nelly looked closer. Some of the lines on the map stood for wide avenues, to be named after the different states.

"And this line, Grandpapa?" she asked, tracing it with her finger. "Is this the grand avenue to be named for Pennsylvania?"

"Yes, Nelly," he said. "The Capitol will stand at one end of Pennsylvania Avenue. At the other end, a home is to be built for our future presidents and their families."

"Won't we ever live there?"

Her grandfather shook his head. James Hoban, an architect recently arrived from Ireland, had designed the mansion, but it would not be finished for several years.

George Washington was President for two terms. The

American people would gladly have elected him for another four years, but he refused. Instead, John Adams, the Vice President, was elected. On March 4, 1797, the day that the new President was inaugurated, many people wept. They did not want George Washington to leave.

Nelly cried too, but on a cold March morning a few days later she felt glad. Seated in the coach beside Mistress Washington, she could see her grandfather riding on horseback beside them. He looked relaxed and contented. For forty-seven years he had been serving his country. Now at last he was going home to stay.

In those days of slow travel over rough roads, the journey from Philadelphia to Mt. Vernon took seven days. On the fifth morning, General Washington and his party reached the Federal City. Nelly had heard so much about the new capital that her first feeling was one of disappointment. Was this place a city? A few large houses were scattered here and there, but most of the buildings were temporary shacks where the workmen lived. The coach jolted and bumped, and bumped and jolted, over a muddy road. This was Pennsylvania Avenue, but it looked more like a swamp. After a while the coachman reined in the horses. The General dismounted and opened the carriage door for Mistress Washington. He held out his hand to Nelly.

To their left, on a gentle slope overlooking the Potomac, a house was going up. The roof was not on, but the light-gray sandstone walls gleamed faintly white in the sunshine. It was going to be a beautiful house, thought Nelly. She smiled up at her grandfather.

"The President's mansion?" she asked.

He squeezed her hand. "Yes, my dear," he said proudly.

If Nelly still had any regrets that she never was to live there, she soon forgot them after her return to Mt. Vernon. "Grandpapa is much pleased," she wrote a friend, "with being once more Farmer Washington."

On his own plantation, which he loved more than any spot on earth, he and Martha settled down to spend the rest of their lives. A few months later they again visited Federal City and saw the President's house. Together they walked through the big unfinished rooms. Beyond the unpainted walls, a city—a city that George Washington had helped to plan—was rising from the mud. It made him happy to know that his dream was coming true.

2 ⃞ *The Grandchildren of John Adams*

During the days when George Washington was still
President and living in Philadelphia, the Vice President,
John Adams, made his home a short distance from the city.
One day Mrs. Adams, seated next to the President at dinner,
was telling him about her grandson who had come down
from New York for a visit. John Adams Smith, aged three,
was a high-spirited youngster, and General Washington
smiled as he listened.

He glanced down at his slice of cake, which was filled with
sugarplums. Digging them out with his knife, he wrapped
them carefully in a napkin. "Please take these to Master

John," he said, "and give them to him with my compli-
ments."

"Thank you, Your Excellency," Abigail Adams replied.
"Johnny will be pleased. He has a likely taste for sugarplums."

Johnny enjoyed the President's treat as much as his
grandmother had expected. Something nice was always happening when he visited his grandparents. Their home,
called Bush Hill, had wide lawns where he could run and
play. Nearly every morning a shepherd brought his sheep
to graze on the lush grass, and Johnny made friends with
the shepherd's dog. But what he liked to do best was to
romp with his grandfather.

John Adams, plump and dignified, had been nicknamed
"His Pomposity," but he was never pompous with Johnny.
He willingly took off his lace-trimmed velvet coat, looped a
rope under his arms, and tied each end to an overturned
chair. Then he got down on his hands and knees. John
Adams Smith mounted the chair and waved a willow switch.

"Get up! Get up!" he shouted, as he urged his make-
believe horse to pull his make-believe carriage.

"Every day after dinner," his grandmother wrote to his
mother, "he sets his grandpapa to draw him about in a
chair . . . to the derangement of my carpet and the amuse-
ment of his grandpapa."

Johnny was one of several grandchildren who frequently
visited the Vice President. Several years after John Adams
became President, Johnny's cousin, Susanna Adams, went
to live with her grandparents. Susanna, at four, was a sweet,
attractive child and only a little less lively than Johnny
himself. Abigail explained to her that they were about to

start on another journey. The capital on the banks of the Potomac was ready.

At least it was supposed to be ready. Ten years had gone by since Congress had voted to build a new city. The six Cabinet officers and their secretaries and clerks arrived there during the summer of 1800. Members of Congress straggled in during the fall. On November 2, John Adams moved into the President's house—the "palace," some people called it—where Abigail and Susanna were to join him later in the month.

As Abigail's carriage passed through Baltimore, she was thinking of several capitals where she had lived in Europe: London, Paris, and The Hague. A new capital in a new nation would be quite different. Most cities grow gradually, but Washington had been carefully planned before any of the buildings were begun. What would the President's palace be like? she wondered. Her husband had merely written that she would have to inspect it for herself. She had been deeply touched by one sentence in his letter: *I pray heaven to bestow the best of blessings on this house, and on all that shall hereafter inhabit it. May none but honest and wise men ever rule under this roof.*

Abigail sighed. John was honest, certainly; honest and brilliant. He had tried hard to be a good president, but he had not been elected to a second term. In four months he and Abigail would be returning to Quincy, Massachusetts. She herself was eager to go home, but she knew that her husband felt deeply hurt.

Glancing down at Susanna, Abigail noticed that she was shivering. The November wind held a cold chill, and she drew the child closer, tucking the carriage robe more firmly

around their knees. The road led through an almost un-
broken forest, and at one place where the road forked the
coachman took the wrong turn. For two hours they were
lost in the woods, but at last they reached Washington City.

Abigail looked around in dismay. There was nothing
about this clearing in the wilderness that was like a city—
except the name. In ten years, she thought indignantly,
much more should have been accomplished. There were a
few more brick houses than when Nelly Custis had passed
through at the end of her grandfather's term. But, like
Nelly, Abigail saw mostly wooden huts. The foundations
for the Capitol had been laid, but only the north wing was
finished. Where were the other beautiful buildings that
Monsieur L'Enfant had planned? Where were the wide
streets and parks?

As the horses floundered up Pennsylvania Avenue, the
carriage wheels sank deep into the mud. A mile and a half
from the Capitol the coachmen drew rein before the palace.
The shacks of the workmen were still standing. The
grounds were littered with rubbish, but the simple gracious
lines of the building itself gave promise of future beauty.
Abigail took Susanna's hand and followed a narrow foot-
path that led around the house. They came to what was
then the main entrance, which overlooked the river. They
walked up some makeshift wooden steps.

The granddaughter looked around, wide-eyed, as she
stood in the doorway. Never had she seen such big empty
rooms! The grandmother sniffed. The plaster was still damp
upon the walls.

The house is upon a grand and superb scale, she wrote
to her daughter a few days later. *I have not a twentieth part*

lamps enough to light it. The fires we are obliged to keep going are another very cheering comfort. But surrounded by forests, can you believe that wood is not to be had, because people cannot be found to cut it! We have indeed come into a new country.

You must keep all this to yourself, and, when asked how I like it, say that I write you the situation is beautiful, which is true. The river is in full view of my window, and I see the vessels as they pass and repass. It is a beautiful spot, and the more I view it the more I am delighted with it.

Abigail knew, as she said in another letter, *This house is built for ages to come.* She refused to be discouraged. There was no fence around the palace yard, and goats and cattle roamed at will throughout the city. She did not dare to hang her laundry outdoors to dry, but she put up a clothesline in the long room that extended across the east end of the building. Later it was to be called the East Room, but it was then a gloomy-looking place, with walls still unplastered. None of the rooms was really finished, but Abigail made six of them fairly comfortable. Enough wood was obtained to keep the fires going in thirteen fireplaces.

In the big oval parlor upstairs she placed the rose damask upholstered furniture brought from the presidential mansion in Philadelphia. Here she served tea when the ladies from Georgetown came calling, and when she and John entertained members of the Congress. Before knocking, their guests often paused outside long enough to scrape their shoes against the trunk of a tree. Even so, much mud was tracked into the palace. Abigail, in her best silk dress, smiled graciously and pretended not to notice.

Susanna, who slept in a small room off her own, was a

great comfort. Soon after her arrival she was taken ill, but when she got better she made the wide cold halls ring with laughter. At the age of four, she already knew her letters, and her grandmother was kept busy telling her stories. After hearing a story a few times, Susanna could usually repeat it word for word.

Many years after, after Susanna had become a grandmother, she also liked to tell stories to a small granddaughter. One of these stories, a true one, was written down by this same grandchild when she grew up.

SUSANNA'S OWN STORY
As told to her granddaughter,
Mrs. C. D. Woods

My grandmother's earliest recollections were of going to Washington and having the whooping cough in the White House. . . . One of her playmates was little Ann Black. On one occasion, my grandmother had received from her Uncle Thomas a present of a doll's tea set, and Ann was invited to "afternoon tea." They had real water in the teapot and cream in the cream jug and sugar in the sugarbowl, and there were cakes on the plates. All went smoothly until my grandmother went out of the room for a few minutes. When she returned, Ann had fled, but the china remained—in little bits on the floor. She had smashed it all. Ann's envy had overcome her friendship.

As toys were more rare in those days than now, this incident produced a coolness between the friends. It lasted until someone gave Ann an extremely pretty but small wax doll, and she invited my grandmother to spend the afternoon with her. My grandmother went, carrying her own doll, and the two little girls played happily together. Ann with proud superiority displayed the advantages of her doll, which was wax and could open and shut its eyes.

But in one unlucky moment, she turned her back. In a flash the wax head was in my grandmother's mouth. Two rows of vindictive little teeth closed through the neck. With a triumphant, "There!" my grandmother put the several parts into Ann's hand and walked out of the house.

She always ended the story with, "And I never was sorry that I bit that doll's head off!"

3 → *A Visit with Thomas Jefferson*

The Randolph children had been hearing about Washington, D.C., from the time they could remember. Their grandfather, Thomas Jefferson, had helped President Washington to make many of the plans for the new city. Now Thomas Jefferson was the President, but he missed his grandchildren. "It is in the love of one's family only," he said, "that heartfelt happiness is known."

In the fall of 1805 he wrote to his daughter, Martha Randolph, and urged her to spend Christmas in Washington. And so she had bundled her own six children and her nephew, Francis Eppes, into her traveling carriage and started out. They did not seem to mind the rough roads, and Mrs. Randolph smiled as she listened to their plans for the holidays.

"Mamma," asked Ann, "will I be old enough to go to a ball this time?"

Ann had been too young to attend grown-up parties when she had visited Washington once before. Two years had passed since then, and she was fifteen. With her lovely auburn hair piled high on her head, she looked almost like a young lady. Her mother peered at her nearsightedly.

"We must wait and see," said Mrs. Randolph.

"Who wants to go to a ball? I'd rather run races on the lawn," scoffed seven-year-old Cornelia. She was thinking of the good times they had had at Monticello, their grandfather's beautiful home in Virginia.

"So would I," said Francis.

"When I was little," nine-year-old Ellen remembered, "I used to sit on Grandpapa's knee and play with his watch chain. But I am too big for that now."

"I'm not too big," said Virginia, who was four.

"I'm not too big," echoed Mary, the youngest.

"I can hardly wait to get to Washington," said Ellen.

"I can hardly wait," Mary repeated.

Jefferson Randolph seemed to think that funny. Mary had not even been born at the time of their earlier visit. Virginia, Cornelia, and Francis had been so young that they had almost forgotten it. But Jeff was thirteen. As the eldest grandson, he held a special place in his grandfather's affections.

It seemed that the journey to Washington would never end. Halfway there the horses were worn out, and the coachman stopped at an inn to hitch fresh horses to the carriage. After four days on the road, he drew rein before the President's house. It had been a long hard trip, but the children forgot that they were tired. A tall distinguished-looking man with reddish hair turning gray stood in the doorway.

"Grandpapa!" they called and ran into his arms.

During the weeks that followed, Thomas Jefferson had his grandchildren with him every moment that he could spare from his duties as President. Virginia and Ellen would lean against his shoulder. Mary and Virginia and Francis would climb into his lap as he went on talking. On one occasion a man who came to call on the President found him down on the floor playing with his small granddaughters. He looked up with a rueful smile.

"Are you a father?" he asked.

"Yes," the startled caller replied.

"Then," said the President, "I need offer you no apology."

The children were enjoying their visit as much as their grandfather. True, the President's house was not as beautiful as Monticello, nor did Cornelia have the races she had wished for. The grounds, with deep holes here and there, were not considered a safe place to play. The President wanted to clear away the rubbish. He wanted to plant trees and shrubs, but Congress had not yet voted to provide the money that was needed to carry out his plans.

The house itself was not yet finished, and there was very little furniture. Most of the rooms looked rather dreary, but in the State Dining Room Martha Randolph noticed eight great silver candelabra which her father had brought from his own home. The light from dozens of wax candles cast a soft glow over the bare walls. The younger members of the family who gathered around the long table were more interested in the dessert.

"Oh!" Everyone from Ann down to little Mary gave a squeal of pleasure. On each plate there was a snowball, or what looked like a snowball. It was ice cream, probably the first ice cream ever served in the United States. Their grandfather had brought the recipe from France. The children dipped their spoons into the small white mounds.

"O—O-oh!" they said again, as the cold goodness trickled down their throats.

Another room that reminded Martha of Monticello was on the second floor. It was here that the President did most of his work. There were bookshelves for his favorite books, and his maps and charts hung on the walls. In the deep window recesses he grew flowers and rare plants, and a mockingbird sang in its cage. The children watched as their grandfather opened the cage door and the bird perched on his shoulder and took food from his lips. Sometimes it was allowed to fly around on the first floor, but it kept its sharp beady eyes on the President. When he returned to his room, it hopped up the stairs after him.

Meanwhile Ann was looking forward to her first ball. She dressed at the home of a friend and looked so different in her grown-up clothes that even Mrs. Randolph did not know her. The children thought this was a great joke.

"My sister excited great admiration on that occasion," Virginia told the story years later. "Her hair was a beautiful auburn, and her complexion had a delicate bloom very becoming to her. My mother was very shortsighted, and seeing my sister on entering the ballroom she asked, 'Who is that beautiful girl?' "

Virginia also told about the time the ambassador from Tunis visited the President. His gold-embroidered jacket was buttoned with real jewels. She never forgot how alarmed she had felt when his secretary leaned over and kissed her. Mary, the golden-haired little sister, received a kiss from the ambassador himself.

All kinds of interesting people came to see Thomas Jefferson, but the most popular visitor was Mrs. James Madison. She was the wife of the Secretary of State and a friend to every member of the family. When Dolley Madison came calling, the young Randolphs gathered around her chair, hoping that she would invite them to go driving. She nearly always did.

"May I run away with the children?" she would ask.

Then they would clamber into her elegant carriage waiting at the door. Down Pennsylvania Avenue they dashed, between the rows of Lombardy poplars that had been planted at the suggestion of Thomas Jefferson. When they arrived at Mrs. Madison's, there was usually a tea party, with cranberry tarts to eat.

One day when the children returned to the President's house, a surprise awaited them. Their grandfather led them into their mother's room. She lay in the big bed, cuddling a small bundle on her arm. As they gathered around her, she pulled back a fold of the blanket.

"A baby!" they shouted.

"Yes, a new brother," their grandfather informed them proudly.

The little brother was named James Madison Randolph. He was the first child born in the building now called the White House.

4 ❧ Friends of Dolley Madison

There were times when the big gray stone mansion seemed ready to overflow with children. Our fourth President, James Madison, had no sons or daughters of his own, and Dolley's son by an earlier marriage was away at school. But she had many young friends, and the three sons and small daughter of her sister Anna were constantly running in and out. Their father, Richard Cutts, was a member of Congress, and they lived only a few blocks away.

One morning, as they were crossing Pennsylvania Avenue to see their Aunt and Uncle Madison, little Dolley fell. As she stood waiting in the hallway, her frock streaked with mud, she could hardly keep back the tears.

"Ah, my sweet!" Dolley Madison, in a dress of simple Quaker gray such as she usually wore in the morning, was coming down the stairs. She took her young namesake by the hand and led the way to her own room. She opened a drawer of her bureau where she kept a supply of fresh clean pinafores for just such emergencies.

"Now let us be tidied up," she said.

After the boys joined them, they gathered around the cage of her pet parrot. When Dolley opened the cage door, he made a sudden swoop and began pecking at little Dolley's feet. When James Madison Cutts walked over to the window, the parrot pounced again and tugged at his shoe buckles. This was repeated with Richard and Walter, who squealed and hid behind their Aunt Madison's skirts. It was a game they often played, and the saucy green bird mimicked their squeals. By the time his mistress put him back into his cage, everyone was laughing.

"Now who would like some cranberry tarts?" she asked cheerfully, and led the way downstairs.

Aunt Madison was always ready to give a party for children and grownups alike. She was such a popular hostess that many of her guests called her Queen Dolley. By 1810 eight thousand people were living in the new capital, and on some evenings it seemed that all eight thousand of them were trying to crowd into the President's house. Congress had voted six thousand dollars to be spent on furniture, and Dolley had used the money to good advantage. She was especially proud of the Oval Room, which had been done over in her favorite color. Yellow satin damask covered the sofas and high-backed mahogany chairs, and there were window draperies to match. She had bought a fine carpet, highly polished tables, and a handsome pianoforte.

Even more elegant than the new furniture were Dolley's clothes on the day of a party. She wore silk and satin gowns with trains that swept the floor. A silk or satin turban covered her dark curls. Usually the turban was trimmed with waving plumes that made her look even taller than she was. Behind her walked James Madison, her "beloved little husband." He was several inches shorter than his wife and wore a plain black suit. When the President was alone with a few close friends, he could relax and tell funny stories, but in a large company he was shy. He was glad that his handsome wife received most of the attention.

One evening a backwoods boy about seventeen years old was attending a reception at the President's house. Having just arrived in Washington, he knew no one. He stood by himself, with his back against the wall, drinking a cup of coffee. Dolley noticed that he seemed lonely, and she walked toward him, her hand outstretched in greeting. He glanced down at his empty coffee cup. What should he do with it? In sudden panic, he thrust it into his pocket, but Dolley pretended not to notice.

"Good evening," she said pleasantly. "And, pray, how did you leave your mother? I have not seen her for some years."

She seemed so interested, as he answered her questions, that he forgot to be embarrassed. When she left him to talk with other guests, he had a chance to take the empty cup from his pocket. Again and again during the evening, he could hear her deep low laugh, and the echoing laughter of her friends. 1085849

On another occasion the Madisons entertained five Osage Indian chiefs at dinner. Leaders of the Indian tribes sometimes traveled long distances to visit their "Great White Father," which was their name for the President. After dinner Dolley returned to her room and sank down on the stool before her dressing table. She was taking off her necklace, when her heart seemed to stop beating for a moment. In her mirror she could see an Indian chief standing behind her. He was watching everything she did.

Dolley tried not to show that she was frightened, as she arose and walked into the hall. There she summoned one of the Negro servants. Together they returned to her room and gently persuaded the Indian to leave.

A young cousin and namesake, Dolley Van Zant, had a more frightening experience. A delegation of Indians happened to be calling on the President on the same day that little Dolley came to see Mrs. Madison. During the afternoon she ran away from her nurse and out into the yard, just as the Indians were leaving. She stood quite still, staring at their feather war bonnets. Their faces were streaked with paint. Never had she seen anyone who looked so fierce.

The Indians stood still, too. Never had they seen such a fat little girl. Her long dark curls were fat, too, like neat sausages hanging around her face. One of the Indians could not resist those curls. Uttering a wild shriek, he dashed toward her, grabbed her by the hair, and raised his tomahawk.

Poor little Dolley did not know that he was only teasing. She uttered a shriek, almost as loud as that of the Indian. Her nurse came running, but it was several weeks before Dolley recovered from her fright.

The older Dolley, although she always appeared cheerful, had troubles, too—much more serious troubles. The War of 1812 had begun. It was a very unpopular war, and many people blamed the President. In August, 1814, the British enemy landed a fleet a few miles down the river from Washington, and there were rumors that the capital was to be invaded. The President was with the militia, which was fighting a battle a few miles away.

The handful of soldiers who were supposed to guard Mrs. Madison had fled, and she was alone except for a few faithful servants. She stood at the window in the stifling heat, looking out on Pennsylvania Avenue. It was clogged with traffic—refugees in carriages and wagons, others on foot—all trying to escape into the country. She was determined not to leave until she received some word from her husband. She wanted to be sure that he was safe.

Finally two horsemen, covered with dust, dismounted at the door. They brought a message from the President. The American militia had been defeated, and the enemy was advancing on Washington. Mrs. Madison must not risk being captured. She was to leave at once and meet him at a certain inn in Virginia.

Dolley's trunks were already packed, not with personal possessions but with important state papers. A friend arrived, begging her to hurry. Still she tarried. A servant was asked to carry her pet parrot in its cage to the home of the French minister. Another was directed to take down the picture of George Washington in the State Dining Room. He brought a ladder and started to remove the screws which fastened the heavy frame to the wall. It proved to be a slow, tedious task, and Mrs. Madison's friend warned her again that there was no time to waste. To avoid cutting the canvas, the servant broke the frame with his fist and took out the picture.

Another carriage stopped at the door. Two refugees, friends of the President, rushed in and asked if they could be of any service. Yes, Mrs. Madison replied. Would they be willing to take the portrait and the state papers she had saved to the Bank of Maryland, where they would be safe from the enemy? Not until she saw the canvas stowed away in the back seat of their carriage, and her trunks securely tied to their luggage rack, would she consent to enter her own carriage.

She was none too soon. The enemy arrived and set fire to the Capitol, the President's house, and other public buildings. That night the sky was bright with the reflected glow, and fires blazed all the next day. The city might have burned to the ground, except for a sudden hurricane with heavy rains that put out the flames. The enemy soldiers had never seen such a storm and were thoroughly frightened. Their commanders feared that American reinforcements might be on their way and ordered a retreat. The refugees began trickling back into the city.

The Madisons were in despair when they saw the public buildings gutted by fire. The President's house was the most seriously damaged, and only the cracked and blackened walls remained standing. All else—the new furnishings of which Dolley was so proud, and her beautiful clothes—had gone up in flames.

The President and his wife found refuge in the Cutts home. He looked pale and tired. Dolley was weeping. Her sister tried to comfort her, and her niece and three nephews stared in surprise. They had never seen Aunt Madison cry before.

"Oh, Anna! Anna!" she sobbed. "Such destruction!"

Then she saw that the children were watching her, and she smiled at them reassuringly. She was thankful that they were safe. Her husband was safe. As for the public buildings that had been destroyed, they could be built again. It would take time, but in a few years there would be a new President's house, rebuilt inside the fire-blackened shell of the old one.

The Madisons moved to Octagon House a few blocks away. Several months later they moved again. Their new home on Pennsylvania Avenue was smaller and not so handsome as Octagon House, but when Dolley entertained she made it blaze with light. It became known as The House of the Thousand Candles.

Meanwhile the war had ended. One night Dolley gave a party for General Andrew Jackson, hero of the recent battle of New Orleans. Men in uniform stood outside the building, holding torches aloft, to light the way for the guests who rode up in their carriages. Negro girls with candles formed a line from the entrance to the mahogany staircase and up the stairs. In the drawing room, fifty other girls stood against the walls, holding a lighted candle in each hand.

The guests pressed forward, eager to meet the grizzled old warrior who was the guest of honor.

This smaller house had certain advantages for the boys

and girls who passed it on their way to school. The walls were set flush with the street. In warm weather the cage of Dolley's parrot hung in an open window on the first floor, and her young friends liked to watch as she fed the saucy green bird. Sometimes she could get him to talk for them.

After the children left, Dolley lingered by the window, listening to the blows of hammers in the distance. She could hear them only faintly. But she knew that four blocks up the street, at 1600 Pennsylvania Avenue, the carpenters were busy. They were rebuilding the President's house. Although she and James Madison would never live there again, it would be ready in time for the next president.

And Dolley Madison was glad.

5 ❧ In the Days of James Monroe
and John Quincy Adams

The President's house was ready and the stone walls painted a gleaming white to hide the stains of the fire. When President James Monroe moved in during the fall of 1817, Maria, his younger daughter, was fourteen years old. She looked up admiringly as she stepped from her father's carriage.

What a lovely white house! she thought.

Even in the days when the mansion was gray, a few people—among them President Madison—had referred to it as "the white house." That was because the gray stone had looked almost white in contrast to some of the red brick buildings close by. Now that it had been given a fresh coat of paint, many people began calling it the White House. Others called it the Executive Mansion, which was to be the official name for years to come.

All of the old furniture had been destroyed by the fire, and new furniture was needed. Much of it was ordered from France, where James Monroe had served as an American diplomat. Maria was entranced by the velvet rugs and taffeta draperies, the shining sconces and chandeliers, the carved tables in gilded wood, the sofas and armchairs upholstered in satin. The East Room was still unfinished, and the story is told that she used it as a playroom.

But not for long! She grew up very fast, and when she was seventeen there was a wedding in the family. Maria was the first daughter of a president to be married in the White House. Her husband, Samuel Gouverneur, was her father's secretary, and the young couple continued to live there.

Nearly everyone was eager to see the rebuilt mansion with its French furniture. The grounds still looked neglected and uncared for, but in 1823 the tall white pillars of the south portico were added.

The following summer General Lafayette returned to American shores. Forty-seven years earlier, as a young man of nineteen, he had run away from France to fight in the American Revolution. He and James Monroe had been wounded on the same battlefield. Later Lafayette had fought for freedom in his own country, and both he and his wife had been imprisoned. Madame Lafayette had been sentenced to die, but James Monroe, who was in France representing the new American government, used his influence to obtain her release. The day that the general called at the White House, he was remembering how much he owed to his old friend.

President Monroe was waiting, surrounded by members of his Cabinet. He, too, had many memories. His thoughts went back to the time when young Lafayette, then called "the boy," had risked life and fortune to help a new nation win its freedom. The sturdy Frenchman who entered the room a moment later, walking with a slight limp, was nearly seventy. The President arose and embraced his guest. There were no words eloquent enough to express the gratitude each felt toward the other.

During the next fourteen months, General Lafayette was the guest of the nation. He traveled through the twenty-four states in the Union at that time. In town after town parades were staged in his honor. Bands played and crowds cheered. Children threw flowers before his carriage, and he received more presents than he knew what to do with. Several times, in the course of his tour, he returned to Washington loaded down with gifts and souvenirs. Part of his collection, including stuffed animals and birds and a model of a steam engine, was stored in the East Room until he could sail for home. He even kept a live alligator there for a while.

During Lafayette's final visit at the White House in the summer of 1825 he was the guest of a new president, John

Quincy Adams. The general had known the President's father, John Adams, during the American War of Independence. He had admired John Quincy, even as a boy. Yet the old French soldier seemed worried. The United States was a republic. Was it wise and right that both father and son should hold the office of president? Did it not make the president seem—well, a little like a king? One day at a White House reception, he turned to Louisa Adams, the President's petite and gracious wife.

"I have been talking with your youngest son," he told her. "A remarkable youth!"

"Thank you, sir." Louisa flushed with pride. Charles Francis Adams, the youngest of her three boys, had just graduated from Harvard College at the age of eighteen.

"Madame, I beg of you," General Lafayette went on earnestly, "do not let *him* entertain thoughts of becoming president."

What a strange remark—and by a gentleman who was usually so courteous, thought Louisa. She felt sure that a brilliant future lay ahead of Charles Francis.

"I beg of you," the general repeated, "do not let him become president, save by the free choice of the people."

Then Louisa understood why he was worried. He had been brought up in a country where kings had ruled only because their fathers had been kings before them. She tried not to smile, as she replied.

"I assure you, sir, that I shall not encourage any such thoughts in Charles Francis."

When the day came for General Lafayette to leave, he and John Quincy Adams stood together on the south portico to say their last good-bys.

"We shall look upon you always as belonging to us . . . as belonging to our children after us," the President told him.

"God bless you," said Lafayette, the tears pouring down his cheeks. "God bless the American people."

He stepped into the waiting carriage. He glanced across the street at the grassy common which people were beginning to call Lafayette Square in his honor. Behind him marched the cavalry that was to escort him to the wharf. John Quincy Adams watched the procession out of sight. He, too, was deeply moved.

Usually he did not like to "exhibit himself," as he once said, and most people found him stiff and hard to talk to. But he unbent with his own family. To his numerous nieces and nephews he was the same kind and considerate Uncle John that he had always been. As President he lived as simply as he had before his election. He arose at five in the morning. He liked to work in the garden, wearing a battered old hat for protection against the sun. And he was always ready to welcome his young relatives to the White House.

"He was not cold as he appeared to the world," said one niece. "He took much interest in all the young persons around him."

The young person who stole the major share of his affection was Mary Louisa, the daughter of his son John. She was the first girl to be born in the White House, and she smiled her way straight into his heart. The President, like John Adams, his father, felt hurt and bitter when he was not elected to a second term. The people, he felt, did not appreciate his long and loyal service to his country. But in the late afternoon, when he visited the nursery, he could forget his disappointment. Looly, as he called the baby, lay asleep in her cradle. Beside her lay Sally, a new doll, a gift from one of her aunts.

As the President stood looking down at them, he was making plans for the future. He looked forward to teaching Looly her letters, but he thought—a little impatiently —that he would have to wait for a while. By the time she was three, she should be able to read from the Bible, he decided. After all, she was an Adams! She was *his* granddaughter! At that moment Looly opened her eyes, and he scooped her up in his arms, doll and all. The baby gave a low gurgle of contentment, and Sally continued to smile out of her painted rosebud mouth.

This doll was a handsome young lady with a body of cloth, a wax head, and a wardrobe made in the latest fashion. More than a hundred years later, as the prized possession of Looly's granddaughter, she made her bow to the people of Washington in an exhibit.

Much had happened during that past century. There were twice as many states in the Union as when John Quincy Adams was President. But Sally, seated in a place of honor, had not changed. The painted black hair was still parted primly in the middle. The rosy cheeks were still pink, and she still smiled her painted smile. The black eyes seemed to twinkle just as they had in the days when she and Mary Louisa lived in the White House.

6 ❧ Andrew Jackson's Houseful of Children

When the President heard little Rachel Jackson fretting in her cradle, he got up and dressed, tiptoed into the nursery, and carried her downstairs. He was wheeling her carriage up and down the East Room when he looked up and saw his daughter-in-law standing in the doorway.

"Father, you shouldn't do that," she protested.

"That's all right," replied the general whose soldiers had nicknamed him Old Hickory. "Rachel likes it, and so do I."

Rachel and her brother, Andrew Jackson 3d, visited the White House every winter. As they grew older, they had wonderful times—and often made a great deal of noise—

romping through the big rooms with their cousins, the four little Donelsons. Andrew Jackson lavished gifts on all of them. When Jackson Donelson was six years old, he was given his own pony. Pennsylvania Avenue had recently been paved, and the boy liked to hear the sound of the pony's hoofs as he went clattering down the street beside the President. A shout went up from the wooden sidewalk, "Hurrah for Old Hickory!"

The men who were cheering wore homespun clothes and waved their coonskin caps. Andrew Jackson was the first president who had come from what was then the western part of the United States. As a boy on the frontier, he had been very poor but had grown up to become successful. To the plain people—those who worked on small farms, in factories, and in little stores—he was a hero. He lifted his hat and bowed.

On his return to the White House he looked with pride on the new north portico, with its tall white pillars. What had once been the back door was now the front door. Pennsylvania Avenue had become such a busy street that callers found it more convenient to enter from that side than from the river. There had been other changes since Andrew Jackson became President. He paused at the door of the East Room. It was now a beautiful room, he thought, with its gilt and cut glass chandeliers and fine new furnishings. It was a room where foreign diplomats, American judges, members of Congress, and his own backwoods followers had been made equally welcome. Several of the children in his family had been christened there.

Just now those same children were having a good time upstairs. There were shouts coming from the nursery, and he knew that the littlest ones would be having their baths. He turned and mounted the steps.

"Watch out, Uncle," cried John Donelson, and Andrew Jackson 3d helped to splash him with water from the tub. There were more shouts when the President of the United States hid behind a chair and pretended to be afraid.

Mary Emily Donelson ran into the nursery and threw her arms around his knees. The President tried not to have favorites, but he called Mary Emily, with her golden curls, "the sunshine of the White House." He looked at her thoughtfully. Down the street a new Treasury building was going up. He had been asked for some souvenir, something precious to him, to be placed in the cornerstone. Taking a pair of scissors, he snipped off one of Mary Emily's curls. Why not give that? he thought. What more precious souvenir could he contribute?

Although Andrew Jackson loved these children like his own, they were not actually related to him. They were the sons and daughters of his wife's nephews. One of these nephews (the father of Rachel and little Andrew Jackson 3d) had been adopted by the Jacksons when he was quite small. The other nephew, Andrew Jackson Donelson, was the President's secretary; and Andrew's wife, the lovely Emily, was his hostess. Their four children (Jackson, Mary Emily, Rachel, and John) lived at the White House. One of Mary Emily's vivid memories when she grew up was of a Christmas celebration with "Uncle Jackson."

ANDREW JACKSON'S HOUSEFUL OF CHILDREN

CHRISTMAS WITH OLD HICKORY
By Mary Emily Donelson Wilcox

The holiday season of 1835 was spent at the White House. For us children it was a very special Christmas, with an unforgettable visit from Sancta Claus. We wondered what he would bring us, how he looked, and where he lived, and we asked many questions of the servants with whom we were privileged pets.

Mammy, a large handsome mulatto, good-natured and domineering, and whom we both loved and feared, said, "I wish to goodness you children would stop talking about old Sindy Klaus. I'd laugh if he got tired of roaming round nights filling stockings. What if he'd stay at home and roast chestnuts by his own fire?"

Vivart, the French cook said, "I no acquaint with Monsieur Sancta Claus; he no live in Paris. In my beautiful France across the blue sea *les petits enfants* never ask questions. They speak only when spoken to."

"Ah ha!" chuckled Mammy. "Mr. Vivart gives you a lesson in manners."

The day before Christmas, we sought out Hans, the German gardener, whose stories about Rhine castles and Black Forest witches and fairies were relished even more than the fruit and flowers he brought upstairs every morning. "I'm sure Kris Kringle will come," said Hans. "He would not forget the White House children. But how I wish you could see the beautiful trees which the boys and girls of Germany trim and light on Christmas Eve. Heaven seems very near at those times."

[49]

At this moment Mammy called us to put on our wraps to go riding with the President. While waiting for him at the front door, George, the coachman, told us of some bad children who had found a bundle of peach tree switches in their Christmas stockings. The switches were wrapped in paper labeled, "To be applied when spanking has proved insufficient." George said that he hoped that we would fare better. Now we had on several occasions come in close contact with peach tree switches, but we did not thank George for reminding us of the stinging experiences.

"To the Orphan Asylum," said the President, on entering the carriage. He often drove there, taking Cousin Rachel, my brother John, and me along. Today there were several packages and a basket of good things on the front seat. The following conversation enlivened the ride:

John: "Uncle, did you ever see Sancta Claus?"

The President (eyeing John curiously over his spectacles): "No, my boy, I never did."

John: "Mammy thinks he'll not come tonight. Did you ever know him to behave that way?"

The President: "We can only wait and see. I once knew a little boy who had never heard of Sancta Claus and he never had a toy in his life. . . ."

The children, quick to detect emotion, felt that some sad memory stirred the old man's heart. We little suspected he was referring to his own childhood.

The President (after several moments of silence): "The best way to secure happiness is to bestow it on others, and we'll begin our holiday by remembering the little ones who have no fathers or mothers."

At the orphans' home, the children gathered in the reception room, and it was gratifying to see their faces light up as he distributed his gifts. His own pleasure was even more gratifying. He lifted a crippled boy in his arms and gave him a jumping jack. "Let's see how this thing works," he said.

The delighted child cried, "Ain't that cute? It hops up and down just like an organ grinder's monkey!"

The day, warm and bright, was more like May than December. The parks, then only grassy commons, were still green. On the way home we called at several houses to leave Christmas souvenirs sent by our mothers. There was a package of snuff for Mrs. Dolley Madison, who was then visiting Washington relatives. There was a hand-painted mirror for Mr. Martin Van Buren, the Vice President, who was reputed to be on very good terms with his looking glass. For other intimate friends there were embroidered handkerchiefs.

After supper we began preparations for hanging up our stockings. Uncle had invited us to use the mantel in his room, and thither we merrily trooped. My brothers, Jackson and John, Cousin Rachel, and I borrowed some of Mammy's stockings. They were very capacious, as she tipped the beam at two hundred pounds. Smaller stockings for the two babies (my little sister Rachel and young cousin Andrew) dangled from curtain rods at the foot of the bed.

Then brother Jackson had a bright idea. "Why not hang up a stocking for Uncle?" he asked.

Running to the bureau, he opened the bottom drawer. He took out a sock and tied it to the fire tongs. "Now let's see how Sancta Claus will treat you, Mr. Uncle Jackson, President of all these United States!" he said.

"Well, well," the old man replied, "to think I've waited nearly seventy years to hang up a Christmas stocking."

Declaring that we were not sleepy, we begged to be allowed to sit up to see Sancta Claus come down the chimney. Then when Mammy hustled us off to bed, we vowed we'd lie awake all night. The next thing we knew it was morning. Mammy's shrill voice was calling, "Christmas gift, you sleepyheads!" We woke up, amazed and indignant to find that we had slept soundly after all. We sprang from our beds.

"Wait till you're dressed," cried Mammy, "or you'll catch your death of cold."

Paying no attention, we raced across the hall to Uncle's room. He was up and dressed and had a bright fire in the fireplace.

"Did Sancta Claus come?" we asked.

"See for yourselves," he said and watched us tenderly as we rushed in to seize our stockings.

All of the stockings, his included, were well filled, and we decided that Sancta Claus was the nicest old fellow in the world. After breakfast we spent the rest of the morning —and a blissful one it proved to be—in the playroom. Our presents included a saddle and bridle, a hobby horse and drum for John, and other presents that we especially desired. Cousin Rachel and I each had a doll and a tea set. My godfather, Vice President Van Buren, sent me a miniature cooking stove with a spirit lamp ready to light. We boiled water in the tiny kettle and popped corn in the oven. There were gleeful shouts when the kettle sang and the corn executed its staccato dance, occasionally giving us a hot smack on face or hands.

One of my presents was so unique that after all these years I still remember it. Madame Serrurier of the French Legation sent me a boy doll wearing a red brass-button jacket, gray gold-striped pants, plumed chapeau, and spurs and saber worn by French postilions. I had had many handsome dolls, but never a boy doll before. Like other foolish mothers, welcoming a son after a succession of disappointing daughters, I clasped him in my arms and crowned him lord and master of my heart.

THE PARTY IN THE EAST ROOM
By Mary Emily Donelson Wilcox

Not the least of that happy day's diversions was getting ready for the afternoon party in the East Room. We had had the fun of delivering the invitations and of selecting the games to be played. When Mammy helped us to get dressed, she outdid herself, rubbing, scrubbing, combing, and curling. We wore the costumes presented to us by our parents as Christmas gifts. Cousin Rachel, who was pretty and graceful, had a pink cashmere; I, a blue one. John was gorgeous in a Highland plaid suit. Brother Jackson, who was tall, erect, and handsome, gave promise in a brass-button jacket of the gallant officer he afterwards became. Mammy changed a bow here, supplied a pin there, and arranged pleats and ruffles. It was amusing to see the high and mighty airs she assumed. When she had finished she stood back and looked us over as an artist might survey a completed masterpiece.

About four o'clock Miss Cora Livingstone, my mother's

dearest friend and the belle of Washington, arrived and led the way to the East Room. When our guests arrived, we children of the President's family met them at the door, kissing the girls and shaking hands with the boys.

The East Room, decorated with evergreens and flowering plants, proved to be an ideal playground. Soon we were romping, scattering, shouting, and laughing, as free and unrestrained as if on a Texas prairie. We played "Blind Man's Buff," "Hide and Seek," "Pussy in the Corner," and several forfeit games. The President, Mrs. James Madison, and a few other older guests watched from the southern end of the room, heartily enjoying our merriment. Mr. Van Buren and Miss Cora joined in some of the games and added greatly to their success.

The Vice President, having incurred a penalty in a forfeit game, was sentenced to stand on one leg and say: *Here I stand all ragged and dirty; if you don't come and kiss me I'll run like a turkey!*

When no kiss was volunteered, he strutted like a gamecock across the room amid peals of laughter.

About six o'clock the band stationed in the corridor struck up the "President's March." Miss Cora formed us into line, the smaller couples leading, and we marched into supper. The dining room was a picture of surpassing beauty. The table was shaped like a Maltese cross, with a pyramid of snowballs in the center. These snowballs were interspersed with colored icicles and surmounted by a gilt gamecock, head erect and wings outspread. Among the other decorations was a tiny frosted pine tree, beneath which huddled a group of toy animals. On the opposite side of the table, a miniature reindeer stood in a plateau of water in which disported a number of goldfish. There were candies and cakes of every conceivable design, and we did ample justice to the tempting repast.

After supper the pyramid was demolished! The snowballs, which were made of noncombustible starch-coated cotton, each enclosing a French pop kiss, were distributed among the children; and we were invited to play "snowball." For some moments the East Room was the scene of an exciting snow flurry, as we pelted one another unmercifully. The snowballs, being soft and light, caused no bruises and inflicted no damage on clothes or furniture. But when they struck, they exploded with a loud noise much like thunder, and we looked like snow-entrapped wayfarers. It was great fun to see the players dodge and to hear them scream, but the game was provokingly brief. The supply of snowballs was soon exhausted.

Then Miss Cora, quietly giving us some instructions, formed us in line again. The band played a lively air, and we marched several times around the room.

"What a beautiful sight," said Mrs. Madison. "It reminds me of the fairy procession in 'Midsummer Night's Dream.'"

The last time we marched around the room we paused before the President. We kissed our hands to him and said, "Good night, General." He smiled and bowed.

7 ❧ *The Young Harrisons and the Tylers, too*

Never had there been a more exciting election than in the fall of 1840. Running against President Van Buren was General William Henry Harrison, called Tippecanoe by his admirers. They still remembered the great victory he had won against the Indians in a battle fought at Tippecanoe, Indiana, many years before. John Tyler of Virginia was the candidate for Vice President, and there was a popular cam-

paign song which ended with the words: *For Tippecanoe
and Tyler, too.*

Perhaps no one sang the song more lustily than did James
and William Harrison, the general's grandsons, who lived
near him in Ohio. It was a proud day for them when he
was elected, and the following February they went with
him to Washington. For James, sixteen, and his younger
brother, William, the journey across the mountains in a
stagecoach was a great adventure. But their biggest thrill
was still to come. They were to see their grandfather inaugurated President of the United States.

Inauguration day was very cold, but people from every
state in the Union had gathered the length of Pennsylvania Avenue. They shouted and cheered as their hero rode
by on a white horse. Again and again he waved his hat, and
his smile seemed to be intended for everyone, even in the
farthest corners of the crowd.

The same unassuming manner and genial wit that had
endeared General Harrison to his friends in Ohio made him
popular in Washington. He enjoyed doing his own market-
ing, and doubtless his grandsons went with him. An old
newspaper clipping, found years later, told of the morning
when "Granny Harrison"—as the people of the opposing
political party called him—bought a cow. It was an experience that two teen-aged boys would have relished.

The farmer who had sold the cow was asked to drive it
to the White House. "You don't mean to say, friend," he
asked, "that you've bought this here beast for Granny
Harrison?"

The President's dark eyes twinkled. He nodded.

"I voted for old Van myself," the farmer went on. "But

the other day at the inauguration, I'll be doggoned—" he laughed heartily—"if I didn't fling my hat into the air and hurrah for Granny Harrison. Couldn't help it somehow."

"Thank you."

The farmer, still not recognizing the President, looked at him narrowly. "What be you at the White House?" he asked. "A gardener? A coachman?"

"Neither. I suppose I may call myself a general servant."

"Do you see much of Granny Harrison?"

"Considerable."

"How do you like the old fellow?"

"Too well, most likely. Well, here we are at the White House stables."

Several men servants, who came forward to take charge of the new cow, touched their hats respectfully. The President turned to his new acquaintance and invited him to breakfast.

"Thank you, I don't care if I do. Say, could you get me a sight of old Granny Harrison?"

"Didn't you see him at the inauguration?"

"Not nigh enough to know what he looked like. I would like to get a squint at him anyways."

The President led the way through the south door and into the family dining room. The farmer, who had probably expected to eat in the kitchen, seemed worried. He looked at the table with its handsome china and silver service.

"I say," he asked. "Granny Harrison wouldn't like this, would he?"

"I think he would, very much. Pray sit down, friend."

The farmer still hesitated, his hand on the back of his chair. "Look here now, ain't you too fresh? Who be you anyhow as makes so bold and takes such liberties in the President's house?"

There was a pause. "The people call me William Henry Harrison," was his reply, "and they have made me President of the United States."

The farmer turned and fled. James and William laughed, but their grandfather was disappointed that his new friend had not stayed for breakfast.

The end of the story neither he nor his grandsons ever knew. As the farmer told it long afterwards, he was so embarrassed that he never stopped running until he was out of sight of the White House. Then he sat down on a curbstone and told himself what an old fool he was.

The Harrison boys had lived in Washington only a month when their grandfather died. For the first time in our history, the Vice President had to take the place of a president. John Tyler was at his home in Williamsburg playing a game of horseshoes with his sons when he saw a foam-flecked horse come dashing down the street. The rider, the Chief Clerk of the State Department, dismounted and handed him a letter. It was signed by the members of the Cabinet. As John Tyler read, his face grew pale.

"What is it, Father?" Tazewell, the eleven-year-old son, asked anxiously.

In a low voice John Tyler explained what had happened. He looked very grave as he thought of his new responsibilities. Before he left for Washington, he called his family together.

"My children," he said, "during the next few years, we are to occupy the home of the President of the United States. Your visitors will be citizens of the United States, and as such are all to be received with equal courtesy. May you never, as the President's family, do aught which you will regret when you shall be nothing higher than plain John Tyler's children."

The two oldest daughters, and their husbands, would continue to live in Virginia. Two younger girls and three sons moved to Washington. The darling of the household was Mary Fairlie, small daughter of the President's eldest son Robert and Robert's dashing young wife, Priscilla.

Priscilla acted as hostess at the White House, the most popular hostess since Dolley Madison. Queen Dolley, as she was still called, had returned to live in a house just across the way, facing Lafayette Square. Although past seventy, she wore her turban with the same air as when she had been a president's wife, and she used rouge and powder to make herself look younger. It was unusual at that time for women to use make-up, and Mary Fairlie stared in amazement the first time they met. But Dolley had a special way with children. She always had a new game to suggest or a new story to tell, and the two became good friends. When Mary celebrated her third birthday, Mrs. Madison was the only grownup invited to the party.

The younger guests came in fancy costumes. One was a flower girl, another was a Greek boy, several were dressed as gypsies. The daughter of a diplomat from Mexico came as an Aztec princess in a satin robe and a blaze of diamonds. Mary Fairlee Tyler, a fairy with gossamer wings, stood beside her mother at the door of the East Room. The diamond star on her forehead sparkled in the light from hundreds of candles. A wand, tipped by another star, was held in her left hand. Her right hand was extended, as she had been taught, to greet her guests.

John Tyler, who stood watching from the doorway, was reminded of what a diplomat from Russia had said. After seeing Mary Fairlee at the White House, he had called her "an empress of a baby." At that moment she looked like an empress—a miniature one—but her grandfather chuckled. He knew that she was not always so dignified.

One day he was hard at work in his study when he was interrupted by a knock at the door. A servant entered. His tone of voice was respectful, but there was a twinkle in his eyes. "Mr. President," he said, "Mrs. Madison is calling."

John Tyler arose from his desk and hurried downstairs. When he reached the reception room, he stopped in surprise. Seated in a big armchair, her feet dangling, sat a pint-sized Dolley Madison. She wore one of her mother's long skirts, with a wide hem hastily made with pins. A scarf was wound around her head to look like a turban. There was a speck of white powder on her nose, splotches of rouge on her cheek.

"Good morning, Mr. President." The voice, though thin and piping, sounded very much like Dolley's.

John Tyler bowed. "Good morning, Mrs. Madison."

He drew up another chair and gravely inquired after his caller's health. The conversation was interrupted by a giggle. Mary Fairlee jumped down, picked up her long skirt, and climbed into his lap.

8 ·♥· *Abraham Lincoln's Boys*

"I wish people wouldn't stare at us so," complained Willie
Lincoln. "Wasn't there ever a president who had children?"

The answer to that question was: "Not for sixteen years."
After John Tyler left the White House five different families
lived there, but they were families of grownups. Then Abraham Lincoln became President. His son Robert was seven-

teen and a student at Harvard. The two younger boys were such lively youngsters that it was no wonder many people were interested in them and wanted to see them.

No longer was the White House a quiet sedate mansion. Within a few hours after Willie and Tad Lincoln moved into their new home, they had explored it from attic to cellar. They dashed through the iron gates and crossed the street to Lafayette Park, where they gazed up at a bronze figure of Andrew Jackson on a prancing horse. "The tippy-toe statue," Tad called it. It probably never occurred to either of the boys that hundreds of statues would one day be erected to their own father. To his sons, he was just "Pa," who comforted them when they were in trouble and did not seem to mind when they got into mischief.

A short time after the inauguration, the War Between the States began. It was a sad time for people in both North and South—and especially sad for the President, who believed that his first duty was to preserve the Union. But the Lincoln boys, although they were homesick at first, were soon enjoying life in Washington. They made friends with the two young sons of Judge H. N. Taft. The Taft boys' older sister, Julia, then sixteen, who shared in many of the good times, later told this story.

THE SHOW IN THE WHITE HOUSE ATTIC
by Julia Taft Bayne

Spring in Washington was never more beautiful than in April, 1861, when my two brothers and I crossed Lafayette

Square on our way to the White House. At my mother's first meeting with Mrs. Lincoln, it had come out that they were about the ages of Willie and Tad Lincoln.

"Send them around tomorrow, please, Mrs. Taft," said Mrs. Lincoln. "Willie and Tad are so lonely, and everything is so strange here in Washington."

Thus began an intimacy between the Lincoln boys and my brothers. Horatio Nelson Taft, Jr., who was called Bud, was twelve, a year older than Willie. Thomas Lincoln (Tad) and Halsey Cook Taft (Holly) were eight. Willie was the most lovable boy I ever knew. Tad had a quick fiery temper, but was very affectionate when he chose. I think there was hardly a day when the four boys were not together.

It was during the following May, as I remember, that Mrs. Lincoln went to New York to buy some furnishings for the White House. She sent a note to my mother, asking that Bud and Holly be allowed to stay with Willie and Tad until she returned. Some days later Mr. Gideon Welles, Secretary of the Navy, told my father that Tad had bombarded the room where a Cabinet meeting was being held, with his toy cannon. President Lincoln had left the meeting to go out and comfort Holly Taft, who had pinched his fingers with some contrivance.

My father was greatly disgusted with these tidings, and I was instructed to go and see that "those young rascals don't tear down the White House." When I reached there, I noticed smiles on the faces of the sentry, doorkeeper, and messengers. I followed that peculiar smile upstairs and asked for the boys. "They are in the attic, Miss," answered a servant, with that same grin on his face.

I ascended to the attic, and as I opened the door Tad

rushed at me, shouting, "Come quick, Julie. We're having a circus. I've got to be blacked up and Willie can't get his dress on and Bud's bonnet won't fit."

The boys had two sheets pinned together for a curtain, behind which was a crowd of soldiers, sailors, gardeners, and servants. Anybody who had five cents could go up the back stairs and see the show.

I took away from Tad the bottle of shoe blacking he was flourishing and made him up with some burnt cork. I told him burnt cork would do just as well as shoe blacking and would be much easier to get off. Willie was struggling with a lilac silk dress of his mother's. Bud was wearing a white morning dress pinned around him in billowy folds. One of Mrs. Lincoln's bonnets was stuck sideways on his head.

"Boys," I said, highly scandalized by these proceedings, "does the President know about this?"

"Yep," said Tad. He began singing at the top of his voice, "Old Abe Lincoln came out of the wilderness."

"Tad, Tad," I remonstrated, "don't sing that. Suppose the President hears you."

"Pa won't care," answered Tad. "I'm going to sing that song in the show."

I had had quite enough and made my escape from the attic. On the stairs I met Major John Hay, President Lincoln's secretary.

"Have those boys got the President's spectacles?" he asked angrily.

"I think they have," I answered. I had just seen them on Tad's nose.

As I went on, Tad rushed after me. "Julie, come back!

Major Hay's taken Pa's spectacles away from us, and we have got to have 'em in the show. That old gentleman who is visiting at your house has two pairs. Make Holly go get 'em."

I disregarded this plea and went on. In the lower hall I met the President, who took my hand and said, "Well, here is Julie come to the circus. Having a great time up there, eh?"

"Yes sir," I said. "They are making a dreadful noise, and they have Mrs. Lincoln's things on, and they look horrid."

He threw back his head and laughed heartily. It was almost the only time I ever saw Mr. Lincoln laugh all over.

"Come, Julie," he said, "let's go up and see it. How much is it?"

"Five cents," I answered. "But, please, I don't want to go. They'll make me help them, and I don't want to. It's horrid of them to wear Mrs. Lincoln's clothes."

Eluding his hand, I went on downstairs. Later Bud told me that the President stayed through the show and seemed to enjoy the boys' jokes. I am glad to remember that hearty laugh of his.

President Lincoln liked to play with the boys whenever he had a little time from his duties. Once I heard a terrible racket in another room. Opening the door with the idea of bestowing some sisterly "don't" upon my young brothers, whose voices could be heard amid the din, I beheld the President lying on the floor. The four boys were trying to hold him down. Willie and Bud had hold of his hands; Holly and Tad sprawled over his feet and legs. The broad grin on Mr. Lincoln's face was evidence that he was enjoying himself hugely. As soon as the boys saw my face at the door, Tad called, "Julie, come quick and sit on his stomach." But this struck me too much like laying profane hands on the Lord's anointed, and I closed the door and went out.

You may infer that I was a conceited little prig. But I really don't think I was. I was dignified with the weight of sixteen years, remember, and many of the pranks of my young brothers and the Lincoln boys deeply shocked my sense of propriety.

I was not the only one thus impressed. I remember the rage of the head gardener, Major Watt, when Tad ate up all of the strawberries being forced for a state dinner. Willie brought the news. His mother said, "Now what made you do that, Tad? Major Watt hoped to have them for the state dinner."

I went out to view the plants. Watt was fuming and threatening to go to Madam.

"The Madam knows it. Willie told her," I said. Then, as he still seemed to be in a great rage, I added, "Tad is Madam's son, remember."

"The Madam's wildcat," snarled the head gardener.

In the fall of 1861, Mrs. Lincoln had a desk and blackboard put into one end of the State Dining Room and secured a tutor. She asked my brothers to study with her boys. I, too, was in and out of the White House every day. President Lincoln always appeared to me well dressed, and he never seemed awkward to me. My father was inclined to be critical in matters of etiquette, but he said he never saw Mr. Lincoln embarrassed in greeting foreigners of distinction.

"The President seemed anxious to make every one comfortable and at their ease," said my father, "which is the essence of good breeding."

The weather that December was quite cold. Willie and Tad had been talking of winters in Illinois, of skating and sledding and snowballing. My brothers listened with round eyes. They had never known the delights of a real snowstorm. They possessed no mittens, no sled, no skates.

"Snow! Snow!" shouted Tad one morning, as some light flakes flew by the window. "That's what I like better'n anything. I hope it'll be over the fences."

To Tad's disappointment, the snowflakes grew more and more infrequent, and at last the sun shone out.

About noon that same day my cousin, Sam Andrus, a soldier in the Union army, and his colonel arrived at our house unexpectedly. As they wished to see the boys, I was sent to bring them home. I went at once to the White House. As I ran up to the sitting room, I almost collided with the tall form of the President, who was crossing the room on the way to the office. He had some papers in one hand, and with the other he stopped my flight.

"Here, here, flibbertigibbet," he said, using the pet name he often called me. "Where are you going in such a hurry?"

"I am looking for the boys."

"Have you looked in the attic, Julie?"

"I am going there now," I said, and left him watching my headlong progress toward the attic, with that quizzical smile I remember so well.

In the attic was a large bin of visiting cards, which apparently had been lately disturbed. There was a nest hollowed out in the center, and the cards were scattered all around the floor. But the boys were not there, so I went home and reported.

After dinner, as the men were enjoying their cigars on the veranda, the four boys appeared. They were dragging a remarkable object which consisted of an old chair on barrel staves and the cover of a Congressional Record nailed to the broken seat. This, they proudly informed us, was a snow sled. But they hung back and seemed uneasy as they were presented to the colonel. Tad and Holly continually rubbed against the veranda railing.

When questioned by Mother, Tad said, "I s'pose it's the snowballs we've got down our backs."

"Snowballs," said Mother in surprise. "Where did you find any snow?"

"Up in our attic," said Tad. "Handfuls and handfuls and bushels and bushels."

Naturally we looked amazed. "Why, Mamma Taft," Willie explained, "Tad's snow is cards. There are bushels in our attic in a big bin, and we throw them up and play it's snowing. There are all the cards all the people have left since General Washington."

"General Washington never lived in your house," said Bud. "The tutor said he didn't."

"Well, there's enough to make a snowstorm without his," said Willie. "Tad and Holly stuffed them down each other's backs like real snow, but the sharp corners stick into us."

Declaring that they couldn't stand it another minute, Holly and Tad went upstairs. The next morning, when I went into the boys' room, I saw in the middle of the card-strewn floor the name of Jenny Lind, the great singer. I picked up this card, and then another and another, and here are the names on some of the "snowflakes" from Tad Lincoln's snowstorm.

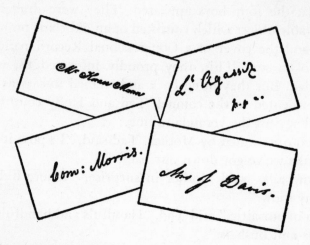

If there was any motto or slogan of the White House during the early years of the Lincolns' occupancy it was this: "Let the children have a good time." Often I have heard Mrs. Lincoln say this with a smile, as her two sons and my two brothers rushed through the room. And no less smiling and gracious was the tall spare man who played with us and told us stories.

When the President came into the family sitting room and sat down to read, the boys would rush at him and demand a story. Tad perched precariously on the back of the big chair, Willie on one knee, Bud on the other, both leaning against him. Holly usually found a place on the arm of the chair, and often I would find myself swept into the group by the long arm which seemed to reach almost across the room.

I wish I could remember some of those stories. Usually they were melodramatic tales of hunters and settlers attacked by Indians. At the close of one favorite tale of frontiersmen chased by the Indians, the President would drawl impressively, "They galloped and they galloped, with the redskins close behind."

"But they got away, Pa, they got away," interrupted Tad.

"Oh, yes, they got away." Then, suddenly rising to his full height, "Now I must get away."

Judge Taft's family moved north in 1863, but in the meantime Willie had died. From then on Tad was the only child in the White House and his father's almost constant companion. Often, when the members of the Cabinet were holding an important meeting, the quiet would be shattered by a loud knocking at the door—three sharp raps followed by two thumps. That was the code Tad had learned in the telegraph office.

"I'll have to let him in," the President would explain to his Cabinet. "I promised never to go back on the code."

There were some people who thought that Tad was spoiled, and they called him "the lovable brat of the White House." One day while he was playing in the attic, he discovered a box fastened to the wall. Inside were the electric switches that controlled all of the bells in the big mansion. He pulled the switches, one after another, to see what would happen. When all of the bells started to ring at the same time, doors began to open. Servants rushed into the corridors. They knocked at the door of the President's study.

[71]

"Did you ring, sir?" he was asked.

"No." He gave the same reply each time. Then he became suspicious. "Maybe you'd better look for Tad," he said.

On another day several ladies on a visit to Washington were walking through the East Room, when they were startled by a sudden clatter.

"Get out of the way!" someone cried.

It was Tad, driving a team of goats hitched to a chair. He dashed in, took a quick turn around the room, and then dashed out again, while the shocked ladies looked on.

Often, when caught in some mischief, the boy bolted into Abraham Lincoln's arms. "You are making trouble for Father," the President would say, or, "My son, can't you manage to make a little less noise?"

Such gentle reproofs were usually all that were needed to make Tad behave.

Mischievous though he often was, he was very tender-hearted. Nearly every day there was a crowd of people waiting to see the President. They sat in the anterooms and lined up on the stairs. Tad, always curious, would go among them, asking what they wanted. One day he saw a poorly dressed woman crying in the corridor. She had come to ask the President to help her husband, who was in military prison.

"I'll ask Pa to get him a pardon," Tad promised, and brushed past the guard who stood outside the door of his father's study.

"All right, Tadpole," said the President. "I'll look into it when I get time."

"But, Pa!" Tad twined his arms around his father's long

legs and refused to budge. "Her boys and girls are hungry. Their pa is shut up in prison, so he can't work for them."

Abraham Lincoln was very busy. But he looked down into the troubled face of his son and promised to see what he could do.

Many people brought their troubles to the President. Sometimes it was the wife or mother or friend of a soldier who came to see him. Perhaps a soldier had disobeyed some army rule and had been sentenced to die. They wanted the President to give the soldier a reprieve or pardon; that is, to write out an order that he was not to be shot. The Secretary of War, Edward M. Stanton, complained that it was bad for army discipline to pardon too many soldiers, but if Abraham Lincoln could find an excuse for saving a man's life he always did.

"Tad tells me I am doing right," he said, with his deep sad smile, "and Tad's advice is usually pretty good."

The following first-hand account of some of Tad's adventures was given by his father's friend, Noah Brooks, a newspaper writer, who was often at the White House.

THE PRESIDENT REPRIEVES A TURKEY
by Noah Brooks

A friend of the Lincoln family once sent a fine live turkey to the White House with the request that it should be served on the President's Christmas table. But Christmas was still several weeks off. In the meantime Tad won the confidence of the turkey, as he did the affection of every living thing with which he came in contact. Jack, as the fowl was called, was fed, petted, and taught to follow his young master.

One day, just before Christmas, 1863, while the President was meeting with his Cabinet, Tad burst into the room like a bombshell. He had just learned that the turkey was about to be killed, and he was crying with rage and indignation.

"But Jack was sent here to be eaten for this very Christmas," said the President.

"I can't help it," roared Tad between his sobs. "He's a good turkey, and I don't want him killed."

The President of the United States, pausing in the midst of important business, took a card and wrote on it an order of reprieve. The turkey's life was spared! Tad seized the precious bit of paper and fled to set his pet at liberty.

On another occasion Tad mounted guard at the foot of the public staircase and exacted toll of all who passed up. "Five cents for the benefit of the Sanitary Fund," he explained to the visitors.

He organized for himself, after the custom of the day, a Sanitary Fair (for the benefit of the soldiers). From a carpenter he secured a pair of trestles and a wide board, which he set up just within the portico of the White House. He had been saving his pocket money and bought out the entire stock of an old woman who sold apples, gingerbread, and candy near the Treasury building. Tad's enterprise was highly successful. But by evening both capital and profits had been spent, and the young speculator went penniless to bed.

Mr. Lincoln took great interest in everything that concerned his son. At night Tad would tell his father all that had taken place during the day. When he finally fell asleep, the weary President turned once more to his desk and worked far into the night. Then, shouldering the sleeping child, he made his way through silent corridors to Tad's bedroom.

One day Tad sauntered into the office of the Secretary of War, Edwin M. Stanton. Mr. Stanton, for the fun of the thing, commissioned him a lieutenant of the United States Volunteers. This elated the boy so much that he managed to get some muskets and began to drill the servants and gardeners. He also procured a suitable uniform and cut quite a military figure.

The President had intended to celebrate Tad's tenth birthday, April 4, 1863, by a visit to the Army of the Potomac, then encamped on the banks of the Rappahannock River, opposite Fredericksburg. Other business intervened, and it was not until after his birthday (and with it the present of a fine pony) that we got away from Washington. The party consisted of Tad, his father and mother, and several others. The soldiers soon learned of Tad's presence in the Army, and wherever he went he divided honors with his father. To men far away from home and their own children, the sight of that fresh-faced laughing boy seemed an inspiration. They waved their hats and cheered like mad.

Later Tad figured in another historic scene. It was the night of April 11, 1863. The news of the fall of Petersburg and Richmond had reached Washington. There was great joy, for we felt that the war was nearly over. On that night the White House was illuminated, and a vast crowd stood outside cheering and shouting with a roar like that of the sea. A small battery from the Navy Yard occasionally rent the air with a salute, and the clamor of brass bands added to the racket in front of the mansion.

Abraham Lincoln was to make a speech, and he and a few friends lingered at the dinner table until it was time to begin. As the little party mounted the stairs to the upper part of the house, roars of laughter could be heard, mingling with the music and the cheers. At one of the front windows, the crowd saw Tad waving a Confederate flag, which had been captured in some battle and given to him. Old Edward, the dignified butler, was struggling with the boy, trying to drag him back from the window.

"The likes of it, Tad!" said the scandalized butler. "The likes of a Confederate flag in a window of the White House! Oh, did I ever!"

The crowd cheered again, as Edward finally dragged the boy away.

Just then the President reached the center window that overlooked the portico. With a beaming face, he looked down on the vast assemblage. Another mighty cheer arose, and then the crowd fell silent.

He began with the words, "We meet this evening, not in sorrow but in gladness of heart." The candles had been placed too low to permit him to see, and a friend who stood behind the drapery of the window reached out and held a candle for him. His speech had been written on loose sheets of paper, and as the President finished with each page he let it fall to the floor. Presently Tad came back and amused himself by chasing the sheets of paper as they fluttered from his father's hand.

"Come, give me another!" he whispered.

The President made a queer motion with his foot toward Tad, but otherwise showed no sign that he had heard.

Below, in that vast sea of upturned faces, all eyes were on the President. Fireworks cast their glow on the tall white pillars of the portico. At the window stood the much loved Lincoln reading the speech that was to be his last to the American people. Behind him, creeping back and forth on hands and knees, Tad was gathering up his father's carefully written pages.

It was well said of him that for several years he gave the White House the only comic relief it knew. His gaiety and affection illumined the darkest hours of the greatest American who ever lived.

9 ⬌ Andrew Johnson's Household

There was the crunch of wheels on the White House drive, and a June breeze stirred the grasses on the lawn. Andrew Johnson's family had arrived from Tennessee. Besides several grownups, there were two sets of grandchildren and his own twelve-year-old son.

"Grandpa! Grandpa!" the younger children cried. "Is this where we are going to live?"

"Yes, my dears," he answered, then helped his invalid wife from the carriage. Several weeks had passed since he, the Vice President, had taken Abraham Lincoln's place. But Mrs. Lincoln had stayed on with Tad, and not until they left for Illinois did the new President move into the White House with his family.

"Yes, this is to be your home," he went on speaking, "and very glad I am to have you here."

The children were bubbling over with questions. Martha Patterson, the older of the President's two daughters, looked at her sister, Mary Stover, and smiled.

The smile faded as they passed through the glass doors into the big bare reception hall and walked from room to room. During four years of war, the house had been thronged with visitors. After President Lincoln died, Mrs. Lincoln had been too ill to pay any attention to what was going on downstairs. Guards had slept on sofas. Soldiers in muddy boots had wandered freely through the parlors. Martha and Mary were shocked when they saw the broken-down furniture and the stained carpets.

Sarah and Lillie Stover, following close behind their mother, found nothing wrong. Their brother Andrew declared that he had never seen such a big house. Belle, Martha's little daughter, was much impressed by the East Room, with its long mirrors and elaborate chandeliers. Andrew Patterson and Frank, the President's son, rushed over to a south window, with a view of the wide lawns sloping down toward the Potomac. Those sunny slopes were not to be resisted.

"Come on, everybody, have a roll," Frank suggested.

With a shout his nieces and nephews followed him outdoors. They threw themselves down on the grass and rolled over and over down the hill.

Later Mrs. Patterson made tea for them in the strangest teapot they had ever seen. It was made of porcelain, like many teapots. But it looked like a railroad locomotive, with the name "Jefferson Davis" on one side. A brass tender, or car, behind the engine held glasses and sugar. Their grand-father explained that this unusual teapot had once belonged to Jefferson Davis, the president of the Confederacy. After the war a friend had bought it at an auction sale and sent it to him.

"How can you make tea on a locomotive?" Andrew Patterson wanted to know.

"You pour the water into the boiler," his mother explained, "and then light this little lamp underneath."

The children gathered around her and watched. As they were waiting for the water to boil, they heard a tinkling little tune. It came from a music box concealed under the tender. Then they heard a whistle. It came from a minia-ture steam whistle on the engine. The water was boiling. The tea was ready.

Mrs. Patterson took glasses from the tender and poured the tea through a spout at the front end of the locomotive. Belle wound up the music box, and as they drank their tea they listened to the rollicking strains of "Dixie."

The next few years were happy ones for the younger members of the family. It never occurred to them that Andrew Johnson was anybody but "Grandpa." If they wanted to see him, they simply bobbed into his office—three or four or five of them—and they were always welcome. He took de-light in bundling them into his carriage and driving off for a picnic in Rock Creek Park. There were stones in the creek, and it was great fun to jump from stone to stone. Sometimes they missed and got wet. Then they would decide that they might as well take off their shoes and stockings and go wading. Before leaving for home, they usually gathered a bunch of flowers for their grandmother, who was ill and seldom left her room.

One day to which the children looked forward every year was Easter Monday. It had long been the custom for the boys and girls of Washington to gather on the Capitol grounds and roll their colored eggs down the grassy slopes. A smaller number came to the White House.

"Then, as now, the celebration of the coming of springtime was considered a great event," said Colonel William H. Crook, a member of the White House staff for many years. "On the afternoon previous, the kitchen would be invaded by the youngsters of the President's family, who would dye dozens of eggs to be put away for the festivities. When the day came the long slopes to the south of the building would be invaded by a host of boys and girls who would roll their eggs down the inclines as their successors do at present. Then the great East Room would be thrown open and many of the children would troop in there for a romp. They would race up and down the great room, singing, shouting, playing games. . . ."

Life in the White House was not all play, of course. Frank attended a boarding school in Georgetown. The others had a tutor. They were expected to study hard and to know their lessons, just as they had at home.

"We are a plain people, sir, from the mountains of Tennessee," Martha Patterson told a newspaper reporter soon after her arrival, "and we do not propose to put on airs because we have the good fortune to occupy this place for a little while."

It was her habit to rise early. There were two cows pastured on the slopes that lay between the house and the river, and she was very proud of her dairy. She armed the servants with mops and pails and saw to it that every nook and corner of the big mansion had a thorough cleaning. When Congress voted a sum of money for new furnishings, she spent the money carefully and wisely. No matter how busy Martha might be in the morning, by afternoon she was dressed and ready to receive callers.

One of the most interesting callers was Charles Dickens. The famous English author had recently arrived in Washington. Every night for nearly a week he read selections from his own books before a large audience. The President bought tickets for every reading, and he invited Mr. Dickens to visit the White House.

When Andrew Patterson learned that he was coming, he wondered if Mr. Dickens would look like Scrooge in *A Christmas Carol*. Or would he look like Mr. Micawber in *David Copperfield*? He and his cousins followed at a respectful distance when Mrs. Patterson showed the visitor through the downstairs rooms. The author's gray beard made him look much more dignified than Mr. Micawber, they decided. And he was too kind to look like Mr. Scrooge. The children liked him.

And he liked the President. In a letter which he wrote to a son in England, he spoke of Andrew Johnson's remarkable face, his courage, and strength of purpose. "I would have picked him out anywhere as a man of mark," he said.

Unfortunately, Andrew Johnson had enemies who did not agree with Mr. Dickens. The President wanted to carry out Abraham Lincoln's policies. He wanted to make it easy for the Southern states to resume their former place in the Union, but there were members of Congress who opposed nearly everything he tried to do. Finally, they voted to impeach him; that is, they tried to have him removed from office. The impeachment trial was held in the Senate and went on for several weeks. Colonel Crook was present in the Capitol the day that the verdict was announced. He sprang down the steps and hurried down Pennsylvania Avenue. A few minutes later he was knocking at the door of Mrs. Johnson's room.

"The President is acquitted!" he cried.

There were tears in Mrs. Johnson's eyes, but her voice was firm. "I knew it. I knew it," she said. "I knew that he would be acquitted, but thank you for coming to tell me."

To friends who came to congratulate Andrew Johnson on his victory, he appeared as calm as he had during the difficult weeks of the trial. Probably no one except his wife and daughters knew how relieved he felt when it was over.

With his family, he could relax, and his chief thought was for their happiness. Toward the end of his term, he celebrated his sixtieth birthday with a gala holiday party for the children. Martha's son Andrew never forgot that evening. Years later he was still telling his own daughter about the flower-bedecked parlors, the chandeliers ablaze with lights, the Marine Band in their bright uniforms, the rollicking strains of the music.

"My daddy often spoke of that children's party," said Andrew's daughter, Margaret Patterson Bartlett, "and I have one of the invitations." The invitation read:

JUVENILE SOIREE
Given by
THE CHILDREN OF THE PRESIDENT'S FAMILY
at the
Executive Mansion
Tuesday evening, December 29, 1868

Nearly four hundred boys and girls lined up in the long hall, and the children's dancing master arranged them in couples. Belle Patterson and Lillie Stover, with their partners, led the promenade into the East Room. There they danced the Polka, the Virginia Reel, and other dances popular in the 1860's. Belle, lovely in billowing hoop skirts, glanced toward the door.

"Why, there's Grandma!" she exclaimed.

Mrs. Johnson stood in the doorway, leaning on the arm of her husband. This was only the second time that she had appeared at any White House entertainment, and her kind gentle face was lighted up by a smile. The short burly President, with the square obstinate chin, was smiling, too.

The Johnson family had a host of friends, including both humble and important people. All alike were sorry when the time came for them to leave Washington. Among many others who came to tell them good-by was Gideon Welles, the Secretary of the Navy.

"No better people ever lived in the White House," he said.

10 ✌ Jesse Grant's Gang

"Our children are going to live and play like ordinary children," Mrs. Grant announced firmly. "Just because they are the President's family, they are not to be constantly on display."

This plan was not easy to carry out with Nellie, the only daughter. Nellie was thirteen when her father, General Ulysses S. Grant, was inaugurated in 1869, but within a few years she had become the belle of Washington. She was beautiful and charming, and the White House was the favorite meeting place for a gay laughing group of young people. The East Room was the scene of many dances and other elaborate parties.

Jesse, who was several years younger, was not interested in

parties. He much preferred to ride Reb, his pet pony, or to play baseball with his friends. "I never considered that my position as my father's son entitled me to any special consideration," he said, "and I know that none of my playmates ever accorded me deference because of that fact. They flocked to the White House because there was the largest and best playground available."

There was a vacant lot south of the big white mansion at 1600 Pennsylvania Avenue. It was on this lot that the boys played ball. Several of them formed a secret club which they named the "K.F.R." The meaning of those mysterious letters no one but the members ever knew, but the President jokingly called it the "Kick, Fight, and Run Society."

In the beginning the K.F.R. met in a tool shed on the White House grounds, with Jesse as the first president. The club had a circulating library and a debating society, and they published a magazine, *The K.F.R. Journal*. The members had many disputes, they got into fights, but they always made up afterwards.

"How we have ever been willing to speak to each other at all, after the way we treated each other in those days, is a wonder," one man recalled. "There were meetings when the president could only keep order by shying kindling wood at the heads of unruly members. Everything happened that could destroy friendship, and yet no friendships have suffered."

Jesse told about the club in a book which he wrote years later. He also told of his experiences as a stamp collector and of other adventures during the days when his father served as President.

MY FRIEND, THE CAPITOL POLICEMAN
by Jesse R. Grant

My life in the White House was that of an ordinary freckle-faced boy, who adored his father and mother, his two older brothers and sister, and was in turn much loved and petted by them. It was in my early days there that I became interested in stamp collecting.

Boys never change. I am convinced that the first cave boy was a collector. The mania for stamp collecting came upon me with the thrill of a great discovery, and for a time it overwhelmed every other interest. No one had ever imagined such a stamp collection as I would gather.

Then I came upon the advertisement of one Anthony J. Foster, of Milk Street, Boston. This advertisement offered a large assortment of foreign stamps for five dollars. I had never possessed five dollars at one time. To me it was a vast sum. It did not occur to me that there was any possibility of acquiring such wealth except by saving it. So I said nothing of my ambition to anyone, save to my cousin, Baine Dent. He and I at once decided that there would be no more candy or soda water until we were possessed of the price of that assortment of stamps.

At last, at the cost of much self-denial, the five dollars was amassed and on its way to Boston. Then, with impatience that reckoned not of distance or train schedules, I looked for the arrival of the stamps. In my anxiety and fear I consulted my stanch friend, Kelly.

Kelly was a big-bodied and bigger-hearted member of the Washington police force, on special duty at the White House. Next to my father he was, in my eyes, the greatest man in Washington.

"Sure, ye better tell your father about it, Jesse," was his advice.

And so I took my trouble to Father.

"What do you wish me to do, my boy?" he asked.

"I thought you might have the Secretary of State, or the Secretary of War, or Kelly write a letter," I suggested.

"Hum-m!" mused Father. "A matter of this importance requires consideration. Suppose you come to the Cabinet meeting tomorrow, and we will take the matter up there."

Promptly on the hour I presented myself at the Cabinet meeting. Hamilton Fish of New York was then Secretary of State, and William W. Belknap of Iowa was Secretary of War. Both were great friends of mine.

"Jesse has a matter he wishes to bring before you, gentlemen," said Father.

Breathlessly I told my story, ending with the suggestion that the Secretary of State, the Secretary of War, or Kelly write a letter.

"This is plainly a matter for the State Department to attend to," said Mr. Fish.

To this Mr. Belknap promptly took exception. He declared it was his intention, as head of the War Department, to act at once.

There followed a general debate, in which the other Cabinet members stood solidly for Kelly. He was declared to have wider powers than the Constitution bestowed upon either the Department of State or the War Department.

When the question was put to vote, Mr. Fish and Mr. Belknap voted for their respective departments. The rest of the Cabinet voted for Kelly. Then the decision was formally announced, and I went downstairs to find him.

I can see Kelly now, as he sat doubled over at a small desk, writing that letter on the stationery of the "Executive Mansion"—so headed at that time—the sweat standing out on his forehead, his great fingers gripping the pen.

At Father's suggestion, I made a copy before mailing the original letter. It read: *I am a Capitol Policeman. I can arrest anybody, anywhere, at any time, for anything. I want you to send those stamps to Jesse Grant right at once. (signed) Kelly, Capitol Policeman.*

A dozen times the following day I made anxious inquiry for the reply to Kelly's letter. In due time the stamps arrived. That five-dollar assortment exceeded our expectations, and for a considerable time my cousin and I were philatelists to the exclusion of all else. One of us conceived the idea of writing to the American consuls for specimens of the stamps of the country to which they were accredited. Many consuls were kind enough to send us full sets. But my joy was considerably dampened by Mother's insistence on my writing a personal letter of thanks to all who responded. I think this requirement had considerable to do with my loss of interest, and the collection of stamps was forgotten. . . .

There were delightfully odd characters among those old White House employees. I spent many contented hours in the stable with Albert, our coachman. If anything could have made Albert unhappy I imagine it would have been a day away from his horses. Often I found him eating his dinner from a tin tray placed upon a stool, and at such times he always carried on a running conversation with the horses and Rosie, his black-and-tan dog. Of the horses, Cincinnati and Egypt were his favorites. Both were beautiful bays, closely matched, splendid specimens of Kentucky thoroughbred stock.

Albert would talk as he ate, but when the last cup of coffee was drunk the procedure was always the same. During all his talk the horses would move restlessly about, answering him with frequent low whinnies. Now, holding a lump of sugar in his lips, Albert would call out:

"Now, you, Cincinnati, you can't have none of this here." Whereupon Cincinnati would walk out of his stall and carefully take the lump of sugar from Albert's lips. The other horses, knowing that their turn was coming, would stamp and paw with impatience.

Another lump of sugar and Albert would say, "Now, you, honey-baby Egypt, wouldn't take no sugar from Albert." And by that time the sugar would be in Egypt's mouth. And so on down the line. All the time Rosie would be lying flat on the floor, her eyes never wavering from Albert's face as she waited her turn. Rosie had no pedigree, but she knew more than any dog I have ever known.

And Albert was the most thoroughly contented man. He was pleased with everything, including himself. Father had bought a great heavy carriage, and the event of the day, for Albert, was when he reined up his four-in-hand in front of the White House. The four wonderful horses dancing and chafing at their bits, the gleaming harness, the great polished carriage, and Albert, his white teeth glistening, made a picture that held every eye. In some mysterious way he could stop the prancing and fretting of his horses at will. The moment that Mother appeared the four would stand like statues. . . .

Grandfather Grant frequently visited us at the White House. The thought of him brings back a disappointment through which I came to a happiness that remains one of my dearest memories. I was nine years old before I attended school, and Grandfather Grant often protested to Father about this, only to meet with the quiet assurance, "School must come soon enough."

One day Grandfather Grant said to me, "When you can write me a letter, Jesse, I am going to give you this gold watch." And he drew from his pocket the enormous hunting-case watch he had carried for many years.

Under the stimulus of this promised reward, I applied myself so diligently that a month later I wrote a letter to Grandfather, reminding him of his promise. That first letter brought a reply, but not the expected watch.

"You are still too young to own so handsome a watch, Jesse," he wrote.

A year later I still remembered Grandfather's promise. I mentioned to Father that I thought I would write to him about it again. It was then a few weeks before Christmas.

"I would not write," said Father. "Wait until you see him."

Then Father at once went to Gault's and purchased a small gold watch. He brought this watch home before dinner that evening and exhibited it to Mother and Nellie, pledging them to secrecy.

"This is Jesse's Christmas present," he explained.

Then, while we were at dinner, Father drew the watch from his pocket and handed it to me.

"Here is your watch, Jesse."

"Why, Ulyss!" exclaimed Mother. "You said that was his Christmas present."

Father turned to me with his slow understanding smile.

"Jesse doesn't want to wait until Christmas, and neither do I," he said.

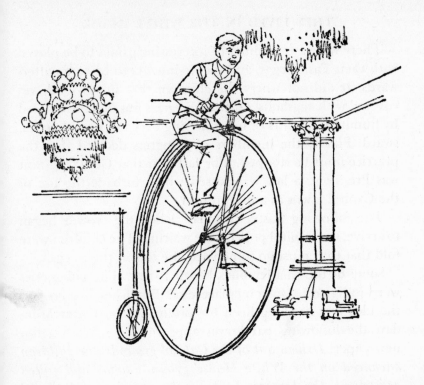

11 ❧ Three Presidents and Their Families

Down Pennsylvania Avenue came the children—girls in starched muslins, some of the smaller ones clinging to the hand of a Negro mammy, and boys of all ages, many well dressed, others in rags. White and colored youngsters mingled in the crowd. Each carried a basket filled with hard-boiled eggs tinted in many colors. For as many years as people in Washington could remember, boys and girls had been going to the Capitol grounds on Easter Monday to roll their eggs down the smooth green slopes.

There were any number of interesting games to be played with their Easter eggs, and picnic lunches to be eaten afterwards. It did not worry the children that the ground was covered with eggshells. Or that the grass was being trampled by hundreds of pairs of feet romping over the smooth green sward. Finally the members of Congress decided that the practice must be stopped. The last year that General Grant was President, a law was passed which forbade the use of the Capitol lawns as a playground.

The following Easter Monday, when the crowds began to arrive, the Capitol police were waiting. The children were told that they must go someplace else to roll their eggs.

Some of the smaller ones began to cry. The older ones were indignant. Go someplace else? But where? Who the idea first has long been forgotten. But on Easter Monday, the following paragraph appeared in a Washington newspaper: *Driven out of the Capitol grounds, the children advanced on the White House grounds today and rolled eggs down the terraces back of the mansion and played among the shrubbery to their heart's content.*

Certainly the slopes back of the Executive Mansion, with a fountain tossing its thin jets of water into the sunlight, were ideal for the annual frolic. It was not the first time that boys and girls had gone there to roll their eggs, but never had they arrived in such large numbers. The new President, Rutherford B. Hayes, and his wife made everyone feel welcome. They had several children of their own, two of whom, nine-year-old Fanny and six-year-old Scott, were still young enough to enjoy a bit of egg rolling themselves. Mrs. Hayes did not realize that they were starting a custom that was to continue through the years.

Another custom was started when a newspaper writer

called her "the first lady of the land." Since that time, the term First Lady has been used for all of the presidents' wives. None of them had ever been more hospitable than Lucy Hayes. The White House always seemed crowded, because she had so many guests. Her son Webb, then twenty-one, never knew from night to night where he might find a place to sleep.

"Cots in the hall, couches in the reception rooms, billiard tables, and even bathtubs had to serve as beds," he said. "When all the others were provided for, I curled up on whatever was left. I considered myself fortunate to sleep on the soft side of a billiard table."

Although Mrs. Hayes liked to entertain, her chief interest was in her family. At the first reception after her husband's inauguration, nine-year-old Fanny was present. She wore a dainty white muslin frock, and her cheeks, flushed with excitement, were almost the same color as her wide pink sash. The high pink boots, of which she was so proud, would seem as quaint to us today as was the "piece" that she recited.

"After President and Mrs. Hayes ended the reception," wrote one newspaper writer, "Fanny sat at the grand piano in the Red Room and, taking off her tiny white gloves, sang to a small audience a funny little rhyme:

> Once there was a little kitty,
> Whiter than snow;
> In the barn she used to frolic,
> A long time ago.
>
> And there was a little mousey
> Running to and fro;
> And the kitty spied that mousey,
> A long time ago.

Two black eyes had little kitty,
Black as a sloe;
And they spied that little mousey,
A long time ago.

Two soft paws had little kitty,
Softer than dough,
And they caught that little mousey,
A long time ago.

Nine sharp teeth had little kitty,
All in a row;
And they bit that little mousey,
A long time ago.

When the teeth bit little mousey,
The little mouse said, Oh!
But she got away from Kitty,
A long time ago.

That first reception was one of the few that Fanny was permitted to attend. "I am obliged to compromise with my little lady," said Mrs. Hayes, "as I found her growing old too fast for her years. We serve her dinner in her room, which she esteems a high compliment."

There were other festivities, planned especially for children, that Fanny enjoyed. At one fancy-dress party she looked her prettiest in a costume as Martha Washington. Scott, her younger brother, went as a soldier.

Rutherford Hayes announced that he did not wish to run for a second term, and he was pleased when his friend, James Garfield, was nominated. The two families knew one another well. Mollie Garfield was an attractive girl of fourteen. The four Garfield boys, ranging in age from sixteen down to nine, were a talented and lively quartet. At the time their father became a candidate, the two older sons were attending a preparatory school in Concord, New Hampshire.

Jim (aged fourteen) is what is called a rollicking boy, one newspaper writer reported. *He is never known to be still unless asleep. He masters his studies almost without effort. At school he excels on the trapeze and the springboard. At home he stands on his head, walks on his hands with his heels up, turns handsprings and somersaults, and jumps the fence in preference to opening the gate.*

Harry (the eldest) is a quiet steady boy. In a characteristic letter he wrote shortly after the convention, he spoke of the fact that some of his schoolmates had manifested a great deal more interest in himself and Jim since their 'pa' was nominated for President. He even thought this a little snobby, and said that he didn't consider that they were a bit bigger or better than they were before, and that he would respect his father just as much 'even if he were nothing but a Congressman all his life.' Evidently Harry didn't seem to think it a very big thing to be a Congressman.

Many newspaper readers laughed when they read those last sentences. But Colonel Crook and others who worked in the White House realized from the moment that the Garfields moved in how much the boys and Mollie loved and respected their parents. They were a scholarly couple. At meals when only the family was present, the President would draw the children out by asking them questions about all sorts of subjects. After their interest was aroused, they would

be the ones to start asking questions, and a spirited dis-
cussion would follow.

Harry and Jim soon returned to their prep school, and
Mollie attended school in Washington. Eleven-year-old
Irvin and Abram, aged nine, studied with a tutor. Abram
showed great talent as an artist. Irvin was the most daring.
At least Colonel Crook thought so.

"One of the first evidences," he said, "that President Garfield's family had taken up their home in the White House
occurred a few days after the new President was inaugurated.
I was walking along the great corridor on the main floor,
when, just as I reached the foot of the grand staircase, I
was startled by a shrill cry of warning.

" 'Hoop-la! Get off the track or you'll be run down!'

"I sprang to one side, and as I did so quickly glanced up-
ward. And there, perched on one of the old-fashioned bicycles with a high wheel, was President Garfield's young son
Irvin, coasting down that staircase like lightning. In an
instant he had reached the foot of it, zipped across the broad
corridor, and turned into the East Room, the flashing steel
spokes of his wheel vanishing like the tail of a comet.

"I stood still for a moment and gasped. That any boy,
even a son of the President of the United States, would dare
to start at the head of that great staircase on a bicycle and
coast down it was almost unbelievable. That he would do
so as successfully as a trained circus performer was beyond
my comprehension. I sprang forward to the door of the
East Room to pick up the dismembered remains of Irvin
Garfield. But it was not necessary. That enterprising American youngster was still on his high wheel. He was treading
it around and around the great East Room with evident

satisfaction to himself, wholly regardless of two or three attendants who stood with their backs as close as they could get to the wall. Their faces were gray with horror and apprehension, as the young human comet went flashing past them.

"Before many weeks had passed by, I got used to such boyish pranks. Every once in a while, when the President was elsewhere and Mrs. Garfield was away, Irvin did not hesitate to bring three or four of his boy friends and their bicycles into the East Room. There they would hold a series of races. The spacious room contained little furniture, and the carpet was firm and smooth, although soft enough to prevent the wheels from skidding. Needless to say, such pranks never came to the knowledge of either President Garfield or his wife, for none of the doorkeepers or servants would tell tales out of school. . . ."

Harry and Jim came home to spend their summer holiday, and all the family was looking forward to taking a trip through New England. They talked about it for days. On the morning of July 2, when it was almost time for their train to leave, one of the doormen with some question to ask was trying to find the President. From above came a shout of laughter, and the doorman hurried up the grand staircase. When he reached the open doorway of the room used by the two older boys, he stopped short in surprise.

Jim and Harry were turning handsprings on the bed, as their father watched.

"I think I can do that as well as you can," he said. Then, to the amazement of the doorman, James Garfield sprang into the air, landed on his hands, and turned a handspring.

"Bravo! Bravo!" the boys shouted.

After James Garfield died, the Vice President, Chester A. Arthur, took his place. He was a handsome kindly man with a grown son, Alan, who was a student at Princeton. Nell, an eight-year-old daughter, moved with her father into the White House. Her mother had recently died, but her Aunt Mary—the President's sister, Mrs. John McElroy—looked after her and made a charming hostess.

"Miss Nellie was brought up in scrupulous retirement," said Colonel Crook. "We saw occasionally a sweet-faced little girl walking or driving by her father's side, or with him in the halls. As far as I know, she was photographed only once. During one of her brother's visits home, he put his little sister, of whom he made a great pet, on a pony and had a picture taken then and there. Once or twice, during the last years of her father's administration, she appeared for a short time at an afternoon reception, dressed in schoolgirl cashmere or muslin. But that was about all the public knew of the family life of President Arthur. For his private affairs he demanded the privacy that any citizen might command."

Although the President tried to shield Nell from publicity, he could not prevent the admiring glances cast in her direction when they went for a drive. Nearly every afternoon, in good weather, he and his daughter stepped into his handsome carriage. The driver on the box lifted his whip, and the horses, a pair of mahogany bays with monogrammed blankets, dashed down the driveway.

As the carriage turned into Pennsylvania Avenue, Nell's dark eyes were bright with interest. The city that she was seeing was very different from the town in which Tad Lincoln and the Johnson grandchildren had lived. Since the inauguration of President Grant, miles of pavement had been laid. Swamps had been drained. Many of the shanties had given place to fine houses. The grand boulevards were lined with trees.

Nell smiled across at her father. Washington was beginning to look like the beautiful capital of which our first President had dreamed.

12 ᤰ Adventures of
the Harrison Grandchildren

The little boy's real name was Benjamin Harrison Mc-
Kee, but "Baby McKee" was the name he was called in the
newspapers. This curly-haired volcano was the grandson of
the new President, Benjamin Harrison, and by inauguration day he had already captured the imagination of the
country. One paper published this bit of doggerel:

Oh Baby McKee! Oh Baby McKee!
Most wonderful babe of our wondrous countree!

Ben was three years old when he went to the White House to live, and newspaper reports kept a close watch on the mansion. They wanted to know what Ben had done the day before, what he was going to do next. They took dozens of pictures of him wearing petticoats and skirts, which were the fashion for small boys in 1889. Sightseers wandered through the grounds, hoping for a glimpse of him. Ben tipped his hat to the gentlemen, as he had been taught, and lifted it for the ladies. Then he went about his own affairs, romping with Dash, his pet collie, or playing with some of his numerous toys.

"Toys of every manufacture and design have been sent to the White House," said one newspaper. "One contrivance was a pony and chaise, complete with harness, lap robe, and whip, and propelled by a marvelous piece of mechanism. Baby McKee rides in his chaise every morning, flourishing his whip over the back of the fiery steed after the example of the White House coachman."

Many of his games he made up. When the chambermaid brought fresh linen for his bed, Ben would often borrow a pillowcase and wrap it around his leg. Then he would limp around the room, pretending to be a wounded soldier. His grandfather had been a soldier, a general—as had his great-great-grandfather, William Henry Harrison—and Ben liked to do whatever "Grandpa" did.

Sometimes he played that he was President and climbed on a stool to make a speech. Again, after watching his grandfather seated in an armchair absorbed in a newspaper, Ben would pull up his own little rocker and pretend to read a paper. There was such a strong family resemblance that he looked like a miniature copy of Benjamin Harrison himself.

The servants could hardly keep from laughing at the sight.

Like many other small grandsons, Ben sometimes took advantage of his grandparents. When told by his nurse that he must take a nap, he regarded her with wide-eyed innocence.

"Grandpa and Grandma never make me go to sleep," he said.

That Ben was not spoiled may have been partly because there were two other youngsters to share the limelight. Also living in the White House was his baby sister Mary. A small cousin, Marthena Harrison, daughter of the President's son, was a frequent visitor. They made a handsome trio, but Marthena was described as "the beauty of the group—sweet and winning, a gentle, quiet little thing. . . ."

Except on state occasions, the children were allowed the run of the mansion, but their favorite playground was the lawn. One day they found a new present there—a billy goat, wearing a bright new set of harness and hitched to a little red wagon. Ben climbed into the driver's seat, and the girls took turns standing behind him, as the goat pulled the cart over the smooth grass. "Never was there such a present!" Marthena recalled.

This enthusiasm was not shared by Willis, the coachman. When he entered the stables the first afternoon, the sad-eyed animal with the long whiskers lowered his head and charged. With the goat in pursuit, Willis made a run for it.

He climbed astraddle the White House fence, according to one newspaper, *near the carriage entrance. But when he attempted to get down on either side, his goatship ran quickly through the gate, prepared to renew the controversy. By this time the White House people were aroused, and two gardeners were dispatched to capture the goat and rescue the unfortunate Willis. The coachman went immediately to the President and presented an ultimatum. Either he or His Whiskers, as he disrespectfully called Baby McKee's billy, would have to go.*

The President did not want to lose his favorite coachman, and a compromise was finally effected. A miniature stable was provided under the rear portico of the Executive Mansion.

The new pet was gentle enough with the children— until the afternoon he ran away. Ben was holding tightly to the reins when His Whiskers dashed into the driveway. Benjamin Harrison, in frock coat and high silk hat, stood on the portico, waiting for his carriage. He gave a startled gasp.

"Stop!" he shouted, but with a defiant toss of the head His Whiskers turned into Pennsylvania Avenue, the red cart clattering along behind him. Behind the cart came a rather stout President, running at top speed and shaking his cane at the disobedient goat. At any moment he expected to see the cart turn over, but he finally caught up with it. Weak with relief, he picked Ben up. Was he hurt? Had he been frightened?

"Why, no, Grandpa." Ben seemed surprised by the questions. He had enjoyed his wild ride.

There were many things about the White House that he enjoyed, and like other Washington youngsters he looked forward to his first Easter Monday. The hundreds of boys and girls who arrived to roll their eggs were surprised to see a new wooden stand on the lawn. It had been erected by order of the President, and members of the Marine Band in their red coats walked across the grass and mounted the steps. The conductor took his place on the platform and raised his baton. The first notes of "Hail to the Chief" sounded on the soft spring air.

A door on the south portico opened. Benjamin Harrison came out with Ben and his two granddaughters. He waved to his hundreds of young guests, and a shout went up that almost drowned the music. Ever since that morning, the Marine Band has played for the crowds that roll their eggs down the grassy slopes the day after Easter.

John Philip Sousa, the band's famous conductor, furnished the music for nearly every public occasion in the White House, including parties for the children. They came to know him well. One day while his musicians were rehearsing in the East Room, he noticed Marthena, standing on tiptoe, trying to watch. At the end of the piece, he lifted her and sat her on the big grand piano. After chatting with her a few minutes, he raised his baton again—and Marthena had an ideal seat for the rest of the rehearsal.

She and her cousins liked living in the White House. Not so their grandmother! It was not nearly so comfortable as her own home in Indianapolis. The carpets were threadbare, the upholstery torn and faded. When she visited the dark damp kitchen, the French chef apologized for the stove.

"I am sorry, Mrs. Harrison," he said. "The range in the White House kitchen, he get hot, he get cold, he never be depend on, and he sometimes smoke. He very old range. He been here since Mr. Johnson. He one poor range."

Mrs. Harrison set to work to put the White House in good condition. Congress voted enough money for repairs and also for electricity. "Ike" Hoover, later to become chief usher, arrived to install the necessary wiring. This new method of lighting was still a novelty.

"The Harrison family was actually afraid to turn the lights on and off," he said, "for fear of getting a shock. The family were even timid about pushing the electric bell buttons to call the servants! There was a family conference almost every time this had to be done. The more rash would touch a button gingerly and jump back."

That same summer of 1891 was an important one for Ben. His parents bought him his first pair of pants, and he felt very proud of his new blue knickerbockers and coat with brass buttons. He resented being called "Baby McKee" more and more as the months passed. Near the end of his grandfather's term, his family prepared to return to Indianapolis. Ben was glad. The prospect of a journey in the railroad cars was exciting. He helped to pack his own small trunk with his favorite playthings.

By the morning of March 4, 1893, all of the trunks were ready. Marthena had already left with her parents, and Ben stood by the window looking out on the grounds white with snow. The trees sheathed in ice sparkled in the sharp winter sunshine. He begged his nurse to let him go outdoors and make snowballs.

There was no time for that. A new baby, wrapped in a long white cloak, was being carried into the nursery. Ruth Cleveland, the child of the next President, was seventeen months old. Mrs. McKee took Ruth on her lap and hugged her. Mary McKee came closer.

"What a pretty locket that baby has on!" she said.

Ben was pleased when he saw how much bigger he was

than the little Cleveland girl. Someone in the room said something about Baby McKee, and he drew himself up proudly. "I am a big boy," he announced. "I am almost six years old."

He was glad that there was a new baby—a real baby this time—in the White House.

13 &~ The Little Cleveland Girls

Among the thousands who saw the inaugural parade in 1893, no one enjoyed it more than did one twelve-year-old boy named Shields Gurley. Much impressed by the brass bands and the marching troops, he was fired with the ambition to be a soldier. Why not form an Honor Guard for Ruth Cleveland, the President's infant daughter, of whom everyone was talking? he decided. Two younger brothers and sixteen of their friends fell in with the plan, and their parents bought each of them a soldier's outfit.

The boys met every day after school and drilled. On the second Saturday in April, when the trees were bursting into leaf, they were ready for their march on the White House. Shields' blue serge jacket had shoulder straps to show that he was a general. He led the way on his pony. Behind him came his two captains on foot, each with eight privates under his command. They carried wooden guns.

Left–right! Left–right! The procession turned into the driveway and came to a halt before the north portico. The captain of Company B marched up the steps and saluted the doorman.

"I have come to see the President," he announced.

The doorman asked the boy to wait. A few minutes later he found himself in the President's study. The big man behind the desk looked up with a smile.

"Good morning," he said. "What can I do for you?"

Again the captain saluted. "Baby Ruth's Honor Guard is waiting out in front," he said. "Would you please come out and review us?"

"I'm sorry, but I am too busy this morning." President Cleveland glanced at the papers piled high on his desk, then at the disappointed captain. "How would you like it," he added quickly, "if Mrs. Cleveland and the baby reviewed you?"

The captain saluted again and hurried outside to report the good news to his superior officer. A few minutes later, Mrs. Cleveland, followed by a nurse carrying the baby, walked out on the portico. Company A and Company B were drawn up in formation before the front steps, and General Gurley wheeled his pony to face his men. He raised his wooden sword.

"Attention! Right dress! Front! Right shoulder arms! Present arms!"

In quick succession the orders came. With a precision that was the result of afternoons of practice, the orders were obeyed. The baby looked on, not knowing what it was all about, but her mother took her hand and waved it. She smiled at the boys. They were smiling, too, when they finally marched off down the driveway, well pleased with themselves and with the First Lady.

Grover Cleveland had been the President once before. During his first term he had married a twenty-two-year-old girl, Frances Folsom. Young and beautiful and kind, she had been a very popular First Lady. During the years that Benjamin Harrison was President, the Clevelands had lived in New York, and it was here that Ruth was born. When her parents brought her to her new home, it seemed that nearly everyone in Washington wanted to see her. The young mother was grateful for the interest, but she soon found that it had an unpleasant side.

There was less privacy in the White House then than became necessary in later years, and people wandered through the south garden as though it were a public park. One day when the nurse had taken the baby outdoors for her daily airing, Mrs. Cleveland was watching from the window.

"Oh!" she gave a sudden gasp of dismay. The carriage was surrounded by a crowd of women. One of them picked Ruth up and kissed her. Soon the baby was being handed from one woman to the next, while the nurse stood by, helpless and in tears.

"From that day," said Colonel Crook, who had served several White House families, "it was impossible for little Ruth to be taken outdoors without having a group of strange women swoop down upon her from all points of the compass. It didn't make any difference if the hour for the outing was changed. The women would be there, waiting for the appearance of the nurse and the baby carriage."

Mrs. Cleveland was distressed and puzzled. She could not

allow Ruth to be fondled and kissed by anyone and everyone, and the President finally ordered the south grounds closed to the public. The results of this order were unfortunate. It was said by unkind people that there must be some reason why they were not allowed to see the baby. Cruel rumors were started that she was a deaf mute and that she was deformed. One day when Frances Cleveland was entertaining a large delegation of women, she saw Ruth toddle past the door.

"Come in, dear," she called. She wanted her callers to see for themselves that her daughter was a normal child—and a very beautiful one.

One day Ruth received a letter from her father's friend, Samuel Clemens. She was too young to know that under the pen name, Mark Twain, he had written such famous books as *Tom Sawyer* and *Huckleberry Finn*. Nor did she understand the meaning of the strange-sounding word "mugwump." This was the nickname for those Republicans who had left their party during the last election to vote for Grover Cleveland, the Democratic candidate.

My dear Ruth, the letter said. *I belong to the mugwumps, and one of the most sacred rules of our order prevents us from asking favors of officials, but there is no harm in writing a friendly letter to you and telling you that an infernal outrage is about to be committed by your father in turning out of office the best consul I know . . . just because he is a Republican and a Democrat wants his place. . . . I can't send a message to the President, but the next time you have a talk with him concerning such matters, I wish you would tell him about Captain Mason.*

In reply Mark Twain received in his mail a tiny envelope. *Miss Ruth Cleveland begs to acknowledge receipt of Mr. Twain's letter,* he read in Grover Cleveland's handwriting, *and to say that she took the liberty of reading it to the President, who desires to thank Mr. Twain for his information and to say to him that Captain Mason will not be disturbed in the Frankfurt consulate. The President also desires Miss Cleveland to say that if Mr. Twain knows of any other cases of this kind, he would be greatly obliged if he will write him concerning them.*

When she was nearly two years old, Ruth was joined by a baby sister. Esther Cleveland was the first child of a president to be born in the White House. A third baby, Marion, arrived while her parents were spending several weeks at their summer home in Massachusetts. The three little Cleveland girls were all born within four years.

Their mother loved flowers, and Ruth and Esther trotted at her heels when she walked through the conservatory carrying Marion in her arms. They listened to her canaries, patted her poodle, and enjoyed the antics of her pet monkey. They wore the embroidered dresses and dainty cloaks that were sent to them, often by people they had never seen. They played with the dozens of toys that came pouring in. They climbed in their father's lap and listened to his stories.

It was rumored that the President was disappointed because he had no son, but no one who saw him playing with his daughters took this seriously. One day a childhood friend of his wife's came to call and asked to see the children. "What a pity that they are all girls," she said.

Frances Cleveland knelt and put her arms around them. "That shows you do not know how nice little girls are," she retorted.

The young mother's letters to her own mother were filled with news of them. She wrote of Marion getting her first tooth and crawling "upstairs quite alone"; of Esther who "is such an odd little pussycat and a great chatterer"; of Ruth "who grows very womanly and helpful." Some of the letters told of the kindergarten which she started for Ruth and Esther and a few of their friends. There were several letters about Christmas. One of the children's favorite gifts was a doll house, a tiny copy of the White House, which their mother had hired a carpenter to make. At the end of Grover Cleveland's term, it was packed to be taken to the new home in Princeton, New Jersey.

Frances Cleveland looked forward to living in a house of their own. At the same time she felt sad to be leaving this gracious mansion to which she had come as a bride. On her final day she sat at one of the south windows looking out on the lawns with a view of the Washington Monument against the blue sky.

"Mamma," asked Ruth, now nearly six years old, "will Papa be just as much my father when he is not President?"

"Yes, dear, even more so," her mother assured her. "Now he is your papa *and* the President. Later he will be all your papa."

Marion wrinkled up her little nose, sniffing the fragrance of the flowers. She was too small when she left to remember the White House. More than thirty years passed before she came back to visit, and then she had a strange experience. She was calling on Mrs. Herbert Hoover, another First

Lady. As she stepped out of the elevator, she seemed to notice a sweet musty scent. Marion looked around, expecting to see roses, but there were none.

"Later I asked my mother about it," she said. "She told me that when we lived in the White House she had always kept roses upstairs. The memory of their fragrance must have come back to me across the years."

14 ⮞ *Theodore Roosevelt's*
Big and Lively Family

Five young Roosevelts sat with their mother in the front row of the Senate Gallery. Down on the Senate rostrum, they could see their father, Theodore Roosevelt. He raised his right hand.

"I do solemnly swear," he said, "that I will faithfully execute the office of Vice President of the United States. . . ."

At the end of the new Vice President's inaugural speech, there was a burst of applause, and no one clapped harder than his children. Afterwards, in the cab that took them to the White House for luncheon, Mrs. Roosevelt glanced at Theodore, Jr., in dismay. He had just arrived from Groton, Massachusetts, where he was attending prep school, and none of his clothes matched. His coat, his trousers, and his vest were three different colors.

"Ted, I wrote you to come in your best clothes," she reminded him.

"I did, Mother." He looked at her indignantly through his spectacles. "These *are* my best; the best coat and the best trousers and the best vest, too."

Mrs. Roosevelt had to laugh.

Meanwhile, Quentin, the youngest member of the family, whose aunt was taking care of him, had arrived at the Executive Mansion. "Quentin," she asked, "do you know what your father is as a result of this morning's ceremonies?"

"Just Father," he replied.

Six months later, President William McKinley died. Theodore Roosevelt became President. Quentin was four years old when he went to the White House to live. Archie (short for Archibald) was seven, Ethel nine. Ted was fourteen. Alice, the older half sister, was a young lady of seventeen. "Princess Alice," as the newspapers called her, was the belle of one party after another. The younger children lived much as they had at Sagamore Hill, their rambling big farmhouse on Long Island. Many a morning began, and many a day ended, with a pillow fight.

"You'd better duck, Father," Ethel or one of her brothers would shout, heaving a pillow in his direction.

Instead of ducking, Theodore Roosevelt, hero of the battle of San Juan Hill during the Spanish-American War,

threw the pillow right back at the culprit. His teeth flashed
in his famous smile. He was having as much fun as any of
the children.

"I don't think any family ever enjoyed the White House
more than we have," he once said in a letter to Kermit.

Much as the younger Roosevelts liked their new home, it
seemed small as compared with the wide acres of Sagamore
Hill. There they had had fields and meadows and barns and
haymows in which to play. One afternoon the President
found Quentin in the south garden, back of the White
House, practicing on a new pair of stilts. The boy walked
through one of the carefully tended flowerbeds.

"Quentin," said his father, "the flowerbeds are not the
proper place to practice walking on your stilts."

Quentin jumped down with a disgusted look. "I don't
see what good it does me for you to be President," he said.
"You can't do anything here."

He soon found that there was plenty to do. He tagged
along after his older brothers when they explored the attic.
They even crawled into the space between the floor and the
ceilings of the rooms below, where only rats had been before. There were noisy games of cowboys and Indians in
the upstairs hall, and the boys flew their kites on the
lawn. Sometimes they pretended that they were soldiers or
knights. Their swords were wooden sticks, their shields the
tops of garbage cans.

An important part of the household were the pets. Jack,
the dog, and Tom Quartz, the kitten, were almost like
members of the family. There were numerous other animals, including rabbits and guinea pigs, squirrels, and rac-
coons. Kermit carried a kangaroo rat in his pocket. Archie's

favorite pet was his spotted pony, Algonquin, not much bigger than a Newfoundland dog.

Once, when Archie had the measles, he missed his pony so much that his brothers decided something had to be done. With the help of a sympathetic coachman, they smuggled it into the basement and then into the White House elevator. Up they went to the second floor and led it along the corridor to Archie's room.

"Algonquin!" Archie called out in surprise, and the pony pricked up his ears.

"Sh!" his brothers whispered, but the secret was soon discovered. Algonquin made a quick trip down in the elevator and back to his stable, but not until there had been a happy reunion with his master.

When Theodore Roosevelt first moved into the White House, he—like our earlier presidents—had his offices on the second floor. There never seemed to be enough space for offices or enough bedrooms for the families. With the coming of six lively children, the upstairs seemed more crowded than ever.

It was finally decided, at the suggestion of the President, that the entire second floor be turned over to his family and that new Executive Offices be built in the western part of the grounds. The old conservatory and greenhouses were torn down, and a terracelike structure was built to connect the new offices with the White House itself. Theodore Roosevelt also brought about another change. The official name for the President's home was still The Executive Mansion. But people had been calling it The White House for many years, and the President had this name engraved on his stationery. By the end of his second term, most people had forgotten that it was ever called by any other name.

Meanwhile his children were growing up. With the three older sons away at school, Quentin was the only one of the boys left at home. Like Jesse Grant, he had a gang. One of the six members had three uncles who had belonged to the K.F.R. thirty-five years earlier. Another member was Charles Taft (called Charlie) who was to live in the White House after his own father, William Howard Taft, became President. A third member, Earle Looker, grew up to write a book about their adventures. The following account is taken from that book.

THE WHITE HOUSE GANG
by Earle Looker

Theodore Roosevelt started the adventurous, rollicking, joyous career of the White House Gang by sending his youngest son, Quentin, to the Force Public School. The arrival of the son of the President of the United States in our dingy red-brick public school occasioned an undeniable flurry among a class of some fifty-odd youngsters who watched with hopeful scrutiny for signs of his being snobbish and stuck-up. But we soon learned that Quentin was like his father and had the same quality of enthusiasm. His little body fairly quivered with impetuosity. His tow head was always mussed, his tie coming untied, his clothes being torn, his stockings refusing to stay up. . . .

For a long time the Gang was unofficial. T.R., the most

active member, was too well known to require describing—
except as we boys saw him. Like the multitude that admired
him from afar, we called him T.R. This was not a gesture of
familiarity; it was not a nickname; we felt he had been
given a title but one man in the world could ever hold. His
active hustling, his bursts of laughter, made us forget anything else about him, in the fun we were having ourselves.

I fully appreciate now—with so many beautiful and historic things stored in the White House—how miraculous
were the accidents *which never happened!* The first "crime"
I remember was directed toward Andrew Jackson, toward
his portrait rather, which hung in the upper hall. Some very
fine shots had been made with spitballs, and very soon Old
Hickory was so covered with them that we dragged a chair
under the portrait to arrange the wet lumps in designs—
three on his forehead, and one on the lobe of either ear. A
poultice of masticated newspaper was set upon the end of his
nose and a gob over each of the buttons on his coat. When
he was finished, Andrew presented a startling appearance,
and we were very proud of our handiwork. But we soon
forgot it, in quest of some more boisterous adventure.

That night, however, in the coolness of White House
sheets—we had been invited to spend the night—our first
exhausted drowsiness was broken by the apparition of T.R.
pulling Q. from the bed and, without the slightest explana-
tion, disappearing with him into the ominous stillness of
an otherwise sleeping mansion.

When Q. returned, he wore a courageous grin but otherwise was much subdued. He reported briefly, that he, per-
sonally, had taken down every spitball from the painted

effigy of President Jackson. In the morning Q. led us before
T.R., who stood sternly before the portrait, rubbing his
glasses vigorously with a handkerchief.

"Who stuck on the first spitball?" he asked fiercely.

Quentin, Charlie Taft, and Dick Chew all voiced confes-
sion together.

"Impossible!" T.R. said, his voice ringing harshly down
the hall. "It's all very sporting to try to take the blame for
one another but I—want—the—truth!"

"I think *I* did," Quentin said.

"You *think!*"

"Yes sir."

"I—I"—he pronounced it *Aiee*—"don't like this!" T.R.
said. "There is some uncertainty, some reluctance. Here is
a case for trial. Oyez! Oyez! This Honorable Court——"

An usher came down the hall with a message for the President. He grinned at all of us, especially at Andrew Jackson.

"Later, later," said T.R. impatiently. "Tell him that I'm
dispensing justice."

The President sat in the armchair directly under the portrait. "Now, the truth of this!" he demanded. "Just imagine
how I would feel, if you rowdies, gangsters, villains threw
spitballs at my portrait!"

This amused Quentin vastly. "You wouldn't mind a bit,"
he said. "Besides, Andrew Jackson doesn't know—he's
dead."

"What? No, I suppose I really *wouldn't* mind. And you're
right, of course, about Jackson's being dead: but how do
you come by the information that he doesn't know? You
can't be sure of that, can you? Moreover, boys, this isn't your
portrait—it belongs to the Government. You're very small

shareholders in it, very small indeed. And in the future, remember, you must not——"

And he read us a vigorous lecture on respect due to property, such as I shall never forget. The finding of the Court was: "Guilty! Altogether guilty!" The sentence: "Quentin may not see any of his friends for one week. You are his friends, so you can't come to the White House for seven whole days." He left us abruptly, his teeth flashing under his mustache, saying over his shoulder as he went: "The truth! The truth! Next time, remember, be quicker with the truth!"

For a moment, we stood in silence before Jackson's portrait. We felt the justice of the reproof and the weight of the punishment. Portraits, henceforth, were taboo. . . .

Theodore, Jr., Alice, Kermit, Ethel, and Archie, the Gang rarely saw because they were older. Theodore, Jr.,—an ancient in our eyes—we once mimicked from the safety of a roof balustrade, because of the bulldog pipe he had brought home from Harvard. We were frightfully short on reverence. There was none we were afraid to mimic—not even T.R.

The ushers may recall how four members of the Gang once squatted on the carpet of the lower corridor, waiting for T.R. to come from his office. Finally he strode down the hall, full steam ahead, oblivious to doors, which always seemed to open miraculously before him. As he passed, we jumped up and followed behind him in single file, mimicking his strenuous pace, arms pumping up and down, our short legs striding as far as they would go. He grinned back over his shoulder and Q., who was directly following, did likewise. The grin passed from boy to boy until it reached me at the end of the procession. I turned and bared my teeth to an usher. We went through two doors in this fashion, which remained open until I had grandly passed through, with my chest swelled out and my head held high. Finally T.R. mounted the stairway with the red-plush rope, and some sudden idea took us elsewhere.

The importance of the President was brought home to me shortly afterwards, in a manner which Q. described as being the most "strikingest." We had been playing in the attic. This was the heaven of the White House. It had great wide spaces and distances; it was crammed full of mysterious stuff. Parts of it were always dark, and these we sometimes explored with flashlights. Better than all, for practical purposes of play, there were cedar chests, some empty, some full, and all smelling of moth balls as well as cedar. It was a thrilling experience, that of opening one of these chests, with only a flashlight to examine its contents.

Several open knife-switches controlled the attic lights. In the late winter afternoons, the place was never wholly light, and it was a favorite trick for someone to "douse the glim" and throw this entire cavern of an attic into utter darkness. The experience was thrilling, because it was scary. Every member of the Gang was afraid to be afraid, and there would be a sort of roughhouse until someone located the switch again.

At times, T.R. would make a break in his official afternoon, in order to play with us. On the occasion I am recalling, he suddenly appeared in his shirt sleeves, his frock coat dangling from his arm. It was our signal for flight. He threw his coat away and chased us, growling ferociously. I was hiding behind a post and beheld Dick Chew closely pursued by T.R. I saw that he was going to be caught. At the same moment I saw the switch. I pulled it; there was immediate darkness, followed by wild shrieks of delight from the Gang. Just then we heard a loud smack. It was that irresistible President striking an immovable post.

"By George! By George!" T.R. bellowed from the center of the attic. "Turn on the lights!"

Proud of my cleverness, I pushed back the switch—to see the President leaning against a pillar, some ten feet away, with his hand over his face. There was a nail in the side of the post, just about the height of his eyes; it was a miracle that he had not struck it. Suddenly, I felt faint.

"When a block of wood *meets* a block of wood, there's bound to be a headache," T.R. said, cheerfully enough. "I'm quite all right. But never, n-e-v-e-r, *never* again turn off a light when anybody is near a post!"

With that, he left us, and went downstairs to bathe his face. Then the Gang descended upon me. I should be punished for my thoughtlessness, and lectured with the new knowledge they—together with myself—had just acquired. I felt the justice of their remarks sufficiently to get fighting mad. My fists flew out, and there was much kicking and hair-pulling until, smothered by bodies, arms, and legs, I was carried, still protesting, to the nearest cedar chest. The Gang threw me into it, shoved me down, and sat on the lid.

At first, the moth balls were pungently pleasant; then things began to get hotter and then hotter, and it was not so easy to breathe. I kicked on the inside of the lid with my toes and hammered away with my fists, to which the Gang responded by drumming their heels on the outside of the chest. I was gasping for air and rather frightened. Inside the chest it was as black as the grave, except for some queer electric flashes before my eyes. I exerted all my strength, trying desperately to lift the lid. The Gang sat tight. I was suffocating!

Suddenly the lid opened, and T.R. looked down into my face. He was quick with his handkerchief, wiping my face, and almost as quick to say, "He's broken out in a sweat! The moth balls have got into his eyes and made them water!" This he said to explain his wiping away my tears, which I thought was fine of him.

"Shutting up boys in cedar chests for more than sixty seconds," T.R. said, "is strictly forbidden—henceforth!"

"Henceforth!" the Gang echoed.

Quentin added, "For evermore!" and swore, "By buzzard!" Buzzard was the great golden eagle, flashing his wings atop the flagpole, which rose from the roof on which we often played.

Somewhere in these upper regions there was a skylight opening, through which we could look down into the main hall of the living quarters, on the second floor. I remember how, from this point of vantage, we once saw Mrs. Roosevelt sitting at a tea table, directly under the skylight. Beside her sat an Italian diplomat, wearing his monocle and balancing his teacup in his hand. The Italian's monocle convulsed us. Our own monocles—crystals from old watches—were promptly brought into service. Thus adorned, we lined up along the edge of the skylight to watch our diplomat and copy his gestures. Quentin—softly at first—began to talk what he fondly imagined to be Italian. The syllables were too contagious for us to remain silent, and soon we were all gibbering away, louder and louder.

[126]

"Quentin!" Mrs. Roosevelt called, and four small boys, each with a glittering monocle in his eye, stared down from the edge of the skylight.

The Italian opened his eyes in astonishment and dropped his eyeglass into his tea! We could not restrain a shout. The Italian threw back his head and laughed with us, and said, "Mrs. Roosevelt, I beg of you to command those monkeys to come to tea, with those things in their eyes."

Later, we watched him drive away, grinning to himself, as Q. said, "like a cheetah," probably very delighted that he had an authentic White House story to tell, even though it was on himself.

15 ⮞ In the Days of Taft and Wilson

Charlie Taft, whose father became President in 1909, had more adventures in the White House before he went there to live than afterwards. He was a member of Quentin Roosevelt's gang—the biggest member and sometimes the pluckiest one, although all of them were plucky enough. Earle Looker, another member, has told a story about a game the boys were playing one day. They were staging what was supposed to be a fight between the Spanish and Americans during the Spanish-American War. Charlie, taking the part of a Spaniard, fell over a chair. Quentin stood over him, brandishing a saber, and accidentally cut Charlie's cheek. When the blood began to flow, the gang was worried. That saber was a valuable relic, and they were not supposed to play with it.

But Charlie was not going to get Quentin into trouble. "Remember, everybody, I fell on a chair," he said.

Quentin raced down the second floor hall to place the saber back over a mantel where it belonged. The other boys smeared some of the blood from Charlie's cheek over the brass feet of a chair. Everyone was discreetly silent when an usher appeared and led Charlie away to Mrs. Roosevelt's room to be patched up.

"Evidently the boy fell against a chair," the usher told her.

If she guessed what had happened she said nothing. The gang could always count on her patience. But one day they were making more noise than even she could stand. She called Quentin into her room and scolded him for roughhousing in the White House.

He smiled at her reassuringly. "It is all right, Mother. Charlie is with us, and it will soon be his house anyway."

Charlie's father was a member of Theodore Roosevelt's Cabinet, and Quentin had heard it said that he would probably be the next president. A year later, after William Howard Taft was nominated, Charlie was interviewed by a reporter. Would he like to be a president's son? the reporter asked.

"Yes, indeed," Charlie replied. "The Roosevelt boys had a fine time in the White House. But I am awfully sorry for Quentin Roosevelt. I do not want him to leave his present home, but he can visit me often."

It was a cold March day in 1909, when William Howard

Taft became President. A blizzard had raged all night, and the inauguration ceremonies were held in the Senate Chambers. The Taft family sat in the gallery, and Mrs. Taft glanced proudly at her children: eleven-year-old Charlie; Helen, who had just won a scholarship at Bryn Mawr College; and Robert, a sophomore at Yale.

The sun had come out by the time the family left the Capitol, and they were able to watch the inaugural parade from the reviewing stand that had been erected in front of the White House. There Charlie ran into his old friend, Quentin, who had cut school in order to be with him. They sat on the same chair to view the long procession, which included cadets from Annapolis and West Point and the Virginia Military Institute, companies of infantry and cavalry, Osage Indians, and Virginia fox hunters in their pink coats. In all, there were thirty thousand people in that parade and sixty bands.

When the new President and First Lady went indoors, they discovered that Charlie already knew how to operate the elevator. Certainly he had used it often enough in the days when he had played with Quentin Roosevelt. He smiled his genial grin, so like his father's, as he offered to take his family upstairs.

During most of his father's term, Charlie attended a prep school in Connecticut, but both he and Robert spent their vacations in the White House. Sometimes when the telephone operator went out to lunch, he allowed Charlie to run the switchboard. A bigger thrill—shared by his older brother and sister—was riding in the White House motorcars. William Howard Taft was the first president to use automobiles instead of carriages.

"Well, children," he said, "enjoy this all you can, for in four more years you may have to begin to walk again."

There were many differences between the customs of 1910 and now. People dressed differently—not only women, but boys. They were usually in their early teens before they put on long trousers. Charlie was still wearing knickerbockers when he came home from school to spend his second summer vacation. One day his sister Helen heard him talking on the phone.

"Certainly not," he said.

A pause. Then Charlie's voice came again, sounding indignant and embarrassed.

"Somebody has been giving you misinformation. . . . An absolute denial. . . . Well, if you want to quote me exactly you may say that I said the rumor is false."

Helen was curious and a little worried. The children of a president must be careful about answering questions concerning their father or the government. She wanted to know who had phoned.

"Charlie admitted that it was a reporter," his mother recalled later, "but he insisted that the subject of his conversation was 'purely personal' and had nothing whatever to do with his sister or with matters of high importance to the government. The question had to be referred to the President before he would admit that the reporter wanted to write something about his going into long trousers.

" 'And if that isn't a personal matter,' said he, 'I should like to know what is.' "

Charlie's legs were beginning to look very long in knickerbockers, however, and a family counsel was held. The time had come, it was decided, to fit him with long trousers.

He was wearing them when he returned to school that fall, feeling every inch a young man.

Helen Taft was able to spend more time at the White House than either of her brothers. After her freshman year at Bryn Mawr, she interrupted her college course to help her mother, and occasionally, when Mrs. Taft was ill, Helen acted as hostess. She enjoyed the interesting round of teas and dinners and the dances in the East Room. She had an even better time at the smaller, more informal parties.

Sometimes she and her friends played "Sardines." The one who was "It" tagged another player, and, after the lights were turned out, both of them would hide in the same place. On would come the lights, and the rest of the group would try to find them. The person who succeeded joined the first two players, and all three had to find a place where they could slip away together. The game went on and on— until only one player was left searching for all of the others. The spacious rooms offered many unusual places to hide, but even so Helen and her friends were packed in "like sardines." The game usually ended in a laugh.

"We are a family that laughs," Mrs. Taft once said. "Both Mr. Taft and the children manage to get some fun out of almost everything."

This was also true of the Wilsons, the next White House family. Margaret, Jessie, and Eleanor, all three, had a sense of humor inherited from their father, Woodrow Wilson. Some of their earliest memories were of him telling funny stories, dancing a jig with a silk hat perched on one side of his head, or reciting nonsense verses. His favorite limerick was:

For beauty I am not a star,
There are others more handsome by far,
But my face I don't mind it;
You see, I'm behind it;
It's the fellow in front that I jar.

According to Eleanor, he considered himself plain, but neither she nor her sisters agreed. They thought him handsome. To them everything he did was perfect, but they had learned to keep their pride to themselves. One day while they were still quite small, their mother came into the nursery.

"Your father has been told that you are boasting about him. Is it true?" she asked.

Eleanor had been too young to understand what the word "boasting" meant. But Margaret had confessed. "Yes, Mother, I do," she said. "I tell them a few things."

"I understand how you feel," their mother replied, "but it does embarrass your father. After this we four will have a beautiful time talking about him as much as we like when we are alone, but not to other people."

The girls had need to remember that advice many times, as the years passed and their father became more famous. In 1913 he was inaugurated President, and they went to live in the White House.

"One of the things I dreaded was the possibility of stiff

pompous servants," said Eleanor, "but the smiling colored
faces that I now saw relieved those fears. 'Ike' Hoover, a
slender dark-haired man who was the head usher, was beaming with hospitality. My first impression of the bedrooms
was that they were terrifyingly large. They were all in
suites, with bedroom, dressing room, and bath. The room
chosen for Jessie and me had enormous old-fashioned ward-
robes, a marble mantel, and great carved gilt mirrors. I
walked through it to the little dressing room beyond and
flopped down on the small white iron bed. 'This is where I
live,' I announced. The little room had simple curtains
with gay flowers, and the carpet was bright blue.

"Mother's and Father's suite, opposite ours, faced south
and overlooked the gardens and the Washington Monument. Their rooms were full of light and air, and there
were fires burning in the open grates. When we ran in to
look, Mother was standing at the window, but she turned
and put her arms around us and said, 'Isn't it lovely, children?' Suddenly I thought, 'This is our home—not the
grand overpowering place I thought it would be.' "

Like Helen Taft, the Wilson girls enjoyed the White
House cars, but there were times when the footman felt
that his dignity was sadly damaged. He sat looking very
prim and proper in his uniform beside the chauffeur. It
was his duty to open the door, but Margaret was usually
too impatient to wait. By the time he could get out of the
car, he would find her standing on the sidewalk. This was
a great joke with her sisters.

"Well, I'm not crippled, am I?" she retorted. "I can
open doors myself—I always have."

Another aspect of the new life that both irked and

amused Margaret was the lack of privacy. Rubberneck wagons drove past several times a day. Often, when the girls were leaving or entering the grounds, they would be pointed out to a busload of eager tourists. It was a startling experience to hear their names being blared through a megaphone, but their sense of humor came to the rescue. They decided to have a turn as sightseers.

"We dressed in old clothes," said Eleanor, "draped veils over our hats, and took a taxi to the bus depot, where we clambered aboard, finding seats in front beside the driver. We were a little worried, for fear we should be discovered, and were very quiet at first, but after a while we recovered our adventurous spirit and began to ask questions. Margaret assumed a high nasal voice and kept up a running fire of comment.

"When we reached the White House, she cried, 'Oh, mister, can't we go in? I want to see where the Wilson girls sleep. Please take us in. . . . Why can't we go in?'

"He soothed her condescendingly and explained that she would have to have a pass. He promised to get it and take her through himself, but for all her pleas he said that she couldn't see the bedrooms. Weak with laughter, I dragged her off as soon as I could."

The two younger sisters were married during their first year in the White House, Jessie to Francis B. Sayre, a young college professor, and Eleanor to James G. McAdoo, a member of her father's Cabinet. The second Christmas after Jessie's wedding, she and her husband returned to spend the Christmas holidays, and early in 1915 Woodrow Wilson welcomed his first grandson into the world.

Francis B. Sayre, Jr., was taken by his parents to their

home in Massachusetts when he was a few weeks old. He grew up without conscious memories of the big white mansion where his grandfather had made history, but in 1952 he came back. By then he was Dean of the National Cathedral in Washington. The White House had just been completely remodeled, and the daughter of another President was showing him through. He asked about the small bedroom off the Rose Room. Yes, it was still there, he was told.

Dean Sayre looked pleased. It was in this room that he had been born—the last baby to be born in the White House.

16 ᘑ The Coolidge Boys

The scene was a tobacco field on a farm near Northampton, Massachusetts, on a day in early August, 1923. A fifteen-year-old boy, busy plucking leaves from the tobacco plants, did not seem to notice the stares of the other laborers. They had read the newspaper accounts of President Warren G. Harding's death—news which had reached the

Vice President while visiting his old family home in Vermont. It was past midnight when he walked into the old-fashioned parlor, lighted by a kerosene lamp. He laid his hand on the family Bible. Then his own father, the local justice of the peace, had administered the oath that made Calvin Coolidge President of the United States.

One of the laborers walked over to the boy. "If my father was President," he said, "I wouldn't work in a tobacco field."

Calvin Coolidge, Jr., looked up, with a suggestion of a twinkle in his eyes. "If my father were your father, you would."

It never occurred to him to quit his job. He had agreed to work in the tobacco field for a certain number of weeks, and he kept his word. His seventeen-year-old brother John had enlisted for the summer at a citizens' military training camp at Fort Devens, Massachusetts, and he continued his training. It was early September before the two brothers arrived at the White House for a visit.

The boys already knew and liked Washington. They had spent several vacations at the hotel where their parents stayed while their father was Vice President. Living at 1600 Pennsylvannia Avenue was quite different. At the time of their first visit—and during several later ones—they took week-end trips down the Potomac in the *Mayflower,* the presidential yacht. In the White House stables they found spirited horses to ride, and there were other interesting animals. Some of these, which arrived from time to time, included a cinnamon bear from northern Mexico, two lion cubs from South Africa, and a wallaby from Australia.

Eventually, these strange gifts had to be sent to the Washington zoo, but the President's cats, Jingles and Tiger, were a permanent part of the household. They wore little collars, on which the President had the words "White House" engraved. Mrs. Coolidge had a devoted Airedale, named Paul Pry because he was so curious. Two beautiful white collies, Rob Roy and Prudence Prim, followed her about the grounds. At last she was living in a house big enough to have all the pets she wanted.

Perhaps no First Lady ever enjoyed herself more than did Grace Coolidge during her first few months in the White House. Especially did she enjoy it when the boys were at home. But one day she made a suggestion that they did not like.

"No, we don't want to go to dancing school," they said emphatically.

"Try it anyway," she urged. "Then you can decide for yourselves."

After they had had a few lessons, she put the question to them again.

"Dancing school?" said John. "It's not so bad."

"What about you, Calvin?"

"Did my father ever take dancing lessons?" he asked.

"No, he never did," his mother admitted.

"Well, if my father never did, I don't need to," he said decidedly.

During the school year both brothers attended Mercersburg Academy in Pennsylvania, but they returned to Washington to spend Christmas. Marion Pollard, a young relative of the President, arrived on New Year's day. Marion, who humorously described herself as "a country cousin," has told this story of her visit.

A "COUNTRY COUSIN" IN THE WHITE HOUSE
by Marion Pollard Burrows

I was thrilled when the invitation came to spend part of my holiday at the White House. On my way to Washington I stopped off in Baltimore to visit a friend, and I phoned Cousin Grace from there.

"Oh, hello, Marion," she said. "I am so anxious to see you, dear. Hurry up and come! Go to the side door and say you are my guest, because if you should go to the front door, they might not let you in. We are having a reception today, and the guards are being terribly strict."

And so I drove up to the side entrance. The doorman, when I told him my name, said, "Oh, yes, Miss Pollard, we have been expecting you."

A maid came, and I was ushered up to my suite. I had a bedroom, bath, and sitting room. There was a fireplace with a little fire blazing away, and on either side was a divan covered with gold damask. To tell the truth, it wasn't a very homey-looking place. The furniture was quite grand, but stiff and formal.

Then John and Calvin, Jr., came in to see me. Their father and mother were receiving callers at the big New Year's reception when the President and First Lady shake hands with everybody. The housekeeper had some luncheon sent up for me, and when I finished, the boys took me downstairs to see the long line of handshakers.

I soon found out that life at the White House, though

lovely and gracious, was exceedingly simple. For years I had
been thinking how wonderful it would be to have breakfast in bed. To be rich enough to have a maid who would
bring me iced orange juice, coffee in a little silver pot, and
everything else in covered dishes, all gay with flowers! When
Cousin Grace's invitation came, the first thing I said to my
mother was, "Breakfast in bed, Mums! Breakfast in bed at
the White House!"

I was reckoning without Cousin Calvin. Do you think
he'd let anybody have breakfast in bed? Well, not unless
one was good and sick—not under his roof!

We had breakfast at quarter to eight, sharp. The family
rooms in the White House are on the second floor. There
is a long hall with rooms on either side. In the morning
Cousin Calvin would be the first one out of his bedroom.
He would pace up and down the hall, watch in hand, waiting for the rest of us. Cousin Grace would come a moment
later—always happy and smiling and looking very neat in
her pretty house dress. Then the boys. And last of all, me.
Cousin Calvin would look at his watch.

"Humph!" he would say. "Quarter of eight, Marion."

Everybody had to be there for every meal. I have heard
Cousin Grace tell about the time that John wanted to go to
a tea dance. He told his father he might be a little late coming home that afternoon and not have time to dress for
dinner. A moment of silence followed. Then Cousin Calvin
spoke.

"You will remember," he said, "that you are dining at
the table of the President of the United States, and you will
present yourself promptly and in proper attire."

I knew, from what Cousin Grace said, that Cousin Calvin

[141]

was not thinking of himself, but of his position. He was the head of a great nation, and he wanted his sons to respect his office as much as he did. Lots of people thought him cold. Well, he was a very reserved person. He was also exceedingly kind, and had a wonderful sense of humor. At night we always ate in the State Dining Room, and I remember the first time that Calvin, Jr., wore a dinner coat. He had forgotten to hitch his tie down in back and it kept riding up, to his discomfort. Presently his father noticed his embarrassment.

"Son," he said, "I know how you can fix that. Get a rope and fasten it on the back there. Then tie a flatiron on each end, and put the flatirons in your coat pocket."

I had always thought that a president's family would lead a very gay life, but Cousin Calvin didn't care for gaiety. They spent almost all of their evenings at home. One night John and I played jazz on the player piano until Cousin Calvin made us stop and sent us off to bed. Another time John managed to get hold of the key of the grand piano in the East Room, and we played all my brother's fraternity songs that we could remember.

Cousin Grace was so smart and stylish that I felt like a little country cousin of the storybooks. She was always very sweet to me. Once she took me to Arlington to see the Unknown Soldier's grave. We drove through traffic like a fire engine. Another day she sent me to Keith's Theater with the best-looking Secret Service man in Washington, and she let me wear her white jade earrings.

Then there was the night that we went to the big charity ball at the Hotel Willard. John was furious because his father wouldn't let him go, but sent him instead to a children's party that afternoon. Calvin didn't mind, but John was seventeen and felt very grown-up.

It was lots of fun dressing for the ball. I had so many frocks I didn't know which one to wear. Several of my friends had insisted that I take along the best of their finery, so that afterwards they could say that their clothes had been to a White House party. I chose a green chiffon that belonged to a girl who was counselor with me at the same summer camp. As I preened in front of my mirror, I decided that girls with red hair should always wear green chiffon.

Cousin Grace was very lovely that night. Her gown had a train, and it made her look tall and dignified. She wore her ermine wrap and loaned me her black velvet. As soon as we reached the ballroom at the hotel, the band began to play *The Star-Spangled Banner*. The dancers fell back, and a pathway was cleared to our box. I tried so hard to look regal that I stumbled and almost fell. I was terribly embarrassed.

There were celebrities everywhere, and I could have stayed forever, just watching and admiring. But after an hour Cousin Calvin said, "It's time to go." Cousin Grace gathered up her train and we all trooped out. Here we'd been all day getting ready. And all for sixty little minutes!

I guess the boys knew that their father would make us come home early. They were waiting up when we arrived, and we sat around and talked and laughed. Before we knew it, it was midnight, and Cousin Calvin said, "Time to go to bed."

I remember that Cousin Grace's birthday came while I

was staying at the White House. I was as poor as a church mouse, but of course I wanted to give her a gift. I asked her that morning if I might go shopping all alone.

Cousin Grace smiled and said nobody who lived in the White House could ever go anywhere quite alone. But she'd send me in a White House car with just the chauffeur and a Secret Service man.

"The photographer is coming this morning," she went on. "John and Calvin, Jr., and I are having pictures taken together. So do your shopping, and we'll all have luncheon together."

I had an awfully nice Secret Service man. I told him I wanted to buy Cousin Grace a gift, and he directed the chauffeur to go to one of Washington's best shops. I walked in and said, "I'd like to see some lingerie." But before I had the words out of mouth, someone had seen the White House car.

"Some lingerie, Miss?" repeated the saleswoman. "Why, surely. We have some delicious little imports."

She started spreading them out—silk and satin and Alençon lace, pleated chiffons, and net that seemed to be almost as fine as cobwebs.

"Oh," I said, "nothing like that!"

"Something for yourself?" she asked.

"No," I said, sticking out my chest. "Something for my cousin. Something for Mrs. Coolidge."

The saleswoman smiled a discreet little smile. "Then won't you let us send a few little pieces? You can make a decision at your leisure, and return the rest."

The Secret Service man nudged me. "Sure," he said, "that's the way."

I gave my name and address, quite proudly. Later that day a truck drove up to the service entrance of the White House and a great number of boxes were delivered to my room. The shop had sent a thousand dollars' worth of lingerie! I took out my purse and counted my money. I put aside enough for my ticket home, and a few dollars for incidentals.

And then I chose a single piece from all that finery. It was all that I had the money to pay for. It cost, I think, about $7.50. I have always wondered what that saleswoman thought when the truck returned. . . . That was the first, last, and only time I ever went to the White House, but the incidents of that one visit remain very vivid.

17 ✌ *The Hoover Grandchildren Meet a Hero*

The third floor of the White House was still called "the attic," but it was not the kind of attic where Tad and Willie Lincoln had once staged their shows. Nor did it bear any resemblance to that vast area of old trunks and chests and mysterious shadows where Quentin Roosevelt and Charlie Taft had played. During the Coolidge administration the roof had been raised and the entire floor rebuilt to provide additional rooms. By December, 1930, three of those rooms had been transformed into a nursery for the use of the grandchildren of Herbert Hoover, the new President.

Peggy Ann Hoover was four and a half—a little girl with shining gold hair. She and her three-year-old brother, Herbert Hoover 3d (called Peter in the family), and baby Joan had arrived from their home in California to stay for several months while their father and mother were away. When they looked down from their nursery windows, they saw trees and bushes hung with icicles that flashed and glittered like ornaments on a Christmas tree. The ground was covered by a soft white carpet—the first snow that Peter and Peggy Ann had ever seen, except on distant mountaintops.

Soon after their arrival, their grandmother helped them into coats and mittens, leggings and boots, and they went for a drive in Rock Creek Park. They watched as she scooped up some of the snow and rolled it between her gloved hands.

"A snowball!" she said, as she held it out for them to see.

Peggy Ann and Peter were delighted when their grandmother showed them how to make snowballs, too. They laughed as they tossed the balls back and forth, and their cheeks tingled with the cold. Washington was not at all like California.

Even Christmas seemed different. On Christmas Eve the Marine Band played as the Hoover family and their guests formed a long procession for the march into dinner. Peggy Ann, the smallest girl, went first, holding the hand of her grandfather, the President. Peter, the smallest boy, was next, marching beside his grandmother, the First Lady. He was half walking, half skipping, by the time he reached the State Dining Room, where he stood quite still for one wonder-filled moment. The large horsehoe-shaped table was lavishly decorated with poinsettias. On a smaller table inside the horseshoe, eight toy reindeer were pulling a sleigh. And in the sleigh sat Santa Claus.

The next morning, the young Hoovers saw a larger Santa —this time a living one. "The old fellow appeared while the household was at the breakfast table," read one newspaper story. "The family had just finished when tinkling sounds like sleigh bells were heard. Mrs. Hoover asked the children if they had noticed, explaining that it might be Santa Claus on his way home to the North Pole. Then the bells came closer and there he was, stepping out of the huge fireplace with a bag of presents on his shoulder.

"Timidly, Peggy Ann and Peter responded to his invitation to come near. Then, reassured, they let him take their hands and walked with him to the end of the room, where he put his bag on the floor. Santa stayed for almost half an hour, chatting gaily and distributing his gifts."

The role of Santa was played by one of the President's secretaries. A mass of evergreens that flanked the fireplace had hidden him from view when he supposedly climbed down the chimney. Peggy Ann and Peter marveled first over the manner of his coming and then over the presents that he kept pulling out of his big pack. There were more toys and dolls and games than any two children could use, and Peggy must have heard some of the grown-up talk about the depression. Many people were out of work that year, and she knew that there were some children who had received no Christmas gifts.

"There are so many things, Santa," she protested, "won't you please give them to some poor little girl?"

Santa agreed, and his pack was still half full when he climbed back into the fireplace.

The next few months passed quickly, and in April Peggy Ann and Peter learned that their parents were returning to the White House. The President and First Lady were expecting several other visitors to arrive on the same day: the king and queen of Siam, and a boy named Bryan Untiedt.

Bryan was a hero. During a recent blizzard in Colorado, the school bus in which he and nineteen schoolmates were riding had been stalled in a snowdrift. Bryan, as the oldest, was left in charge while the driver went for help. For a day and a half he had struggled to keep his friends alive. He set them to fighting and boxing with one another, because he knew that if they stopped moving they might die in the bitter cold. He stripped off his own clothes, down to his underwear, and gave them to his younger brother. When finally rescued, he was taken to the hospital to recover from exposure and from frozen hands and feet. President Hoover was so impressed by the young hero's cool-headed courage that he invited him to visit the White House.

It was Bryan's thirteenth birthday, and he was still in the hospital, when he learned of the invitation. "Gee, won't that be great?" he said. "It's sure been a swell birthday."

Three weeks later Bryan was well enough to begin his journey. It was his first ride in a Pullman. When he got off the train in Washington, grasping his small cardboard suitcase, he was met by a Secret Service man. He was whisked away in a big car to the White House, and an hour later he was talking with Mrs. Hoover in her upstairs sitting room. She was a tall dignified woman with silvery hair, and at first he felt shy. Then she told him a funny story, and once he started laughing he forgot to be embarrassed. He seemed completely at ease—as calm as during the Colorado blizzard —when he was introduced to the President.

Herbert Hoover, after a long talk, asked him what he would like to see.

"I read that you have a lot of dogs here," the boy replied. "I think I'd like to see them first."

In the kennels Bryan counted nine dogs, ranging from Shamrock, the big wolfhound, down to a miniature poodle named Tar Baby. He picked up the terrier puppies, one by one, and petted them. He had noticed the tall shaft of the Washington Monument only a block or so away. After leaving the kennels, there was time for a short walk to see the monument close up. Bryan climbed the 898 steps to the top, where he saw the shining white city spread at his feet. From that height the White House looked like a toy White House, and the river was blue and sparkling in the noonday sun.

Before luncheon, members of the family and several house guests assembled in the Red Room. "When the President arrived, they arose according to custom," said Ike Hoover, the chief usher. "Not Bryan Untiedt, however. Presidents coming into the room meant nothing in his young life, and he just watched from his seat on the big red sofa. It was amusing to see him, entirely composed, hold his chair, when everyone else rose as if by magic. I walked over to him and with a soft word put him right. There was a smile on the faces of President and Mrs. Hoover as the latter walked over to him and led him to the dining room, seating him next to the President."

Bryan's visit lasted for four days, and each day was filled with sightseeing. He went to the Capitol and saw the Supreme Court judges in their long black robes. He spent several hours at George Washington's home at Mt. Vernon. In the Arlington National Cemetery, he watched the impressive ceremony of the changing of the guard before the Tomb of the Unknown Soldier. Back in Washington, he toured the Bureau of Engraving and saw how money was printed. The superintendent allowed him to hold a big ream of paper bills, representing many thousands of dollars. During his visit to the Smithsonian Institution, he stood for a long time before the airplane in which Charles Lindbergh had made the first solo flight across the Atlantic.

"It doesn't look as big somehow as I thought it would," he said. "I don't see how he ever got across the ocean in it."

In the meantime Bryan and the Hoover grandchildren had become good friends. They visited the kennels together and played with the dogs. When Mrs. Hoover took them to Rock Creek Park for a picnic, Bryan built an outdoor fire to cook their lunch. When they returned to the White House, he showed the children the harmonica he had brought with him.

"Music of a kind hitherto unheard in the White House echoed through the lower apartments of the mansion," one newspaper reported. "Mrs. Hoover and several guests, wondering where the tuneful strains came from, went on a hunt for the musician. In a corner they found Bryan Untiedt, entertaining the grandchildren of the President with a harmonica recital. Peggy Ann and Peter were jumping up and down in a spontaneous dance, while Bryan played "Lone

Cowboy," "Red Wing," and "Oh, Dem Golden Slippers." The arrival of Mrs. Hoover and her guests did not dismay him. He kept right on playing."

After this story was printed, people began sending Bryan harmonicas. By the fourth morning, when he was packing to leave for home, he had a large collection, ranging from instruments two inches long to a big two-decker harmonica nearly a foot across. His small cardboard suitcase was too small to hold them—and all of the other gifts that he had received—and he was provided with a leather suitcase almost as big as a trunk. It contained two new overcoats and presents for every member of his family. Mrs. Hoover was sending Mrs. Untiedt a tablecloth, and Bryan had bought her a dressing gown. As a joke he was taking Mr. Untiedt a cigar made of rubber, but he also had a real present for his father. This was a pen-and-ink set made from wood which had been salvaged when the White House was undergoing repairs.

When Bryan reached the railroad station, a Secret Service man put him on board the train. As he stood on the step, he was surrounded by reporters asking him questions.

"What impressed me most?" he replied. "Well, I never saw anything before like the White House."

A month later the Hoover grandchildren also left Washington, but they came back the following December to spend another Christmas. This year Peter and Peggy Ann were host and hostess at a big party. The guests, instead of receiving gifts, were asked to bring them. They arrived laden with toys and candy and warm clothing, which were turned over to a "Mrs. Santa Claus" in the State Dining Room. She and her helpers set to work at once to pack them in big boxes to be shipped to a mining town in West

Virginia. Most of the miners in this town had been out of work for a long time, but now their families were assured of a merry Christmas.

The next morning, Mr. Santa again visited Peggy Ann and Peter. He came down the chimney, as he had the year before. His pack was filled with toys, most of them from the ten-cent store. This time Peggy did not need to ask him to take some of the gifts to children who otherwise might not have any presents. Mrs. Santa had already attended to that the day before.

18 ᴥ *The Grandchildren of F.D.R.*

In the White House, as in other American homes, Christmas has usually marked the high point of the year's festivities, but there probably have never been any gayer celebrations than in the time of Franklin D. Roosevelt. "I never knew people who loved Christmas the way the Roosevelts did," said Mrs. Henrietta Nesbitt, their housekeeper. "All the five-ring-circus excitement of the past year seemed to gather to a point in the White House and explode in a lather of tinsel stars."

It was a big and affectionate family. Soon after the father was inaugurated in 1933, one of his sons made a surprising discovery. He was returning home from a party one night when he was stopped at the gate. The guard was polite but firm. Did he have a pass to get in? The son had to wait until someone could be found who could identify him.

"What kind of place is this, anyway," he asked his mother the next morning, "where you can't get in when you are living here?"

The two younger boys were still attending prep school at Groton. The three older children were married, and James and Elliott each had a small youngster. The only daughter, Anna Roosevelt Dall, brought her two children to the White House to stay. Not since their distant cousin, Theodore Roosevelt, lived there had the newspapers printed so many stories about the younger members of a president's family.

"Sistie" and "Buzzie" (as Anna Eleanor and Curtis Dall were nicknamed) had a jungle gym in the south garden, and pictures of it appeared in many newspapers. When they went to the circus and shook hands with a famous clown, or when they walked with their grandmother among the Easter egg rollers on the lawn, people read about it from coast to coast.

Easter Monday, like Christmas, seemed to take on a special flavor while their grandmother, Eleanor Roosevelt, was First Lady. She arranged for Howard Thurston, a magician, to entertain the children; and there was a very real-looking menagerie on the lawn, with mechanical animals operated by electricity. Sistie, aged six, wanted to see them close up. Her brother, not yet three, clung to his mother.

Buzzie drew back in alarm, read one newspaper account, *when the papier-mâché elephant waggled its ears and the lion roared. His mother reassured him, and then he smiled as the boa constrictor reared its head and the trick tiger crouched in its cage as if to spring.*

After returning to the shade of the south portico, Sistie and Buzzie met Mr. Thurston. He waved his wand over their heads. "Every child has an egg in his mouth on Easter," he said.

He held his hand under Buzzie's mouth—and there was an Easter egg! He reached inside Buzzie's sweater and pulled out a live rabbit, which he gave to Sistie.

"Just a moment," Mr. Thurston assured her brother, "and I'll find one for you!"

Again he put his hand inside Buzzie's sweater. Out came a second rabbit, nose wiggling, eyes blinking, and the magician placed it gently in Buzzie's arms.

There was always something happening in the big white mansion on Pennsylvania Avenue. Sistie and Buzzie would stand at an upstairs window, their noses pressed against the glass, watching the long succession of cars swing around the driveway. One never knew who would be coming to call, and the children received a great deal of attention. After a while this became rather tiresome. It was embarrassing to have people stare at them. No matter where they went, there seemed to be a photographer trying to snap their pictures. When their grandmother commissioned an artist to paint their portraits, neither of them liked the idea.

Buzzie sat quietly through the ordeal, but Sistie thought

of various ways to make it more interesting. She jumped around. She whirled back and forth in the playroom swing. She even stood on her head.

"The only way I could get her at all was by making her in little bits," the artist said. "I made sketches of her eyes, nose, and mouth separately. It wasn't that she meant to be unpleasant. It's simply that she had had her picture taken so many times that she did not like to pose."

Meanwhile other granddaughters and grandsons were being added to the family. Within a few years they numbered thirteen, and they were constantly coming and going. "Sistie and Buzzie were there the most, and people knew them best," said Mrs. Nesbitt, "but the others were just as sweet. There were cribs, high chairs, and perambulators all over the White House, and kiddie cars, tricycles, and scooters were parked outside under the stately *porte-cochère*. There was a slide on the lawn, and children racing about, and dogs barking. They were nice children, uninhibited and friendly."

Those were years of crushing responsibilities for the President, and Eleanor Roosevelt was almost as busy. Yet they found time to play with the youngsters. Mrs. Roosevelt often dictated letters holding a baby on her lap. Sometimes she got down on her hands and knees and pretended to be a bear. Again she was a bucking bronco, allowing a small grandson to ride on her back. A game which the younger ones liked to play with the President was called "Whiffen-poof." His hand became a mysterious bug that traveled— and traveled—and finally pounced, amid the delighted shrieks of the small fry seated on the side of his bed while he had his breakfast tray.

"The grandchildren were the only ones allowed in Franklin's room while he ate his breakfast," said Mrs. Roosevelt, "and occasionally I had to rescue him from the little darlings. Once I heard much noise and calls for help and, on going to his room, found two little girls, Sara (James's oldest child) and Chandler (Elliott's little daughter) jumping up and down on his bed, shouting at the top of their lungs, 'He's my grandfather!' 'No, he isn't, he's mine!' Franklin sat trying with one hand to protect his breakfast tray from being swept off the bed, and holding the telephone in the other. 'Wait a minute,' he was saying desperately to the operator, 'I can't talk to Paris just yet.' "

In spite of an occasional inconvenience, the President and his wife doted on their ever-increasing younger generation. They also became very fond of Diana, the daughter of Harry Hopkins, the President's friend and adviser. After Mrs. Hopkins died, Mrs. Roosevelt brought the little five-year-old daughter home with her.

Diana lived at the White House for nearly five years, which was longer than any of the grandchildren. After breakfast she was often seen—a friendly brown-eyed child with glints of red in her brown hair—roller-skating on the concrete walk in front of the Executive Offices. Sometimes her friends were invited for a dip in the President's swimming pool. On several occasions Mrs. Nesbitt caught her chasing the guards with lipstick, trying to paint mustaches on their faces. The guards seemed to enjoy the game as much as Diana.

Once she had a long talk with Winston Churchill, the Prime Minister of England, who was visiting at the White House. "We talked mostly about geography," she explained. Another time Mr. Churchill brought her a doll for a Christmas present.

She was quite casual about the many famous people that she met until she learned that King George VI and Queen Elizabeth were coming. Her idea of a queen came from her fairy tales. Would Elizabeth wear a crown? she wondered. Would she carry a scepter? Diana became so excited that Mrs. Roosevelt decided to tell the queen about her. Her Majesty, who had two young daughters of her own, smiled and nodded. She suggested that Diana be presented to her that evening.

"Diana was a solemn little girl," said Mrs. Roosevelt, "and she was speechless when the king and queen came down the hall. She made her little curtsy to each one and when they asked her questions she managed to answer, but her eyes never left the queen. After it was over I said, 'Does she look as much like a fairy queen as you expected?' With a little gasp she said, 'Oh, yes!' And she did, for the queen's spangled tulle dress, with her lovely jewels and her tiara in her hair, made her seem like someone out of a storybook."

After the royal couple had departed to have dinner at the British Embassy, Diana found her father waiting for her downstairs. "Oh, Daddy," she said breathlessly, "I have seen the fairy queen!"

As the months passed, Diana became accustomed to meeting royal visitors, including several near her own age. It was once said of Mrs. Roosevelt that "she collected children." She entertained many unfortunate ones who had never been to a party before. The royal children who were her guests from time to time were unfortunate, too, but for different reasons. World War II was being fought in Europe. Several royal families, driven from their own countries, had found refuge in North America.

Among others, Princess Juliana, later to become queen of The Netherlands, and her two young daughters were guests of the President and the First Lady. In 1941 the Crown Princess Martha of Norway and her three children spent Christmas with them and shared in the family tree on the second floor. Princess Astrid and Diana were in the group that stood on the portico, watching the ceremonies when the tall municipal tree in the south garden was lighted.

"By this time," said Mrs. Nesbitt, "I was accustomed to the simple manners of royalty, but Princess Martha was the most informal. The children went in and out, like normal healthy children, not at all like little princesses in exile. Only, they were not gay like our American children. None of these exiled people were gay."

That Christmas had overtones of sadness for exiles and Americans alike. The United States had entered the war. We were still at war three Christmases later. Franklin D. Roosevelt had been elected for the fourth time, and inauguration day on January 20, 1945, marked the beginning of his twelfth year in office—a longer period than any other president had ever served.

The ceremonies were very simple, because of the war. There were no marching bands, no parade up Pennsylvania Avenue. Instead of taking the oath of office at the Capitol, the President stood on the south portico of the White House. Instead of tens of thousands of spectators, as in other years, there were only a few thousand.

Among them were his grandchildren. The eldest was an attractive, fair-haired girl of seventeen, looking almost grown-up in a black frock. This was Anna Eleanor, who as a little girl had been called "Sistie." Beside her stood her fifteen-year-old brother Curtis, once known as "Buzzie." The others ranged like stair steps, down to the youngest who was about three.

The war was nearing an end, and it was an historic occasion. Franklin D. Roosevelt wanted his grandchildren— all thirteen of them, the largest number of any of our presidents—with him on that day.

19 ↝ Margaret Truman, College Girl

When Margaret Truman was a little girl living in Independence, Missouri, she decided that some day she was going on the stage, perhaps to be an opera singer. Then her father was elected Senator and her family spent part of each year in Washington, where Margaret attended a private school. After her graduation she talked over her ambition with her parents.

Senator Harry S. Truman looked pleased. He played the piano, and he liked music as much as his daughter did. "I'm tickled you're thinking of music," he told her. "But first, baby, I want you to go to college and get your degree."

He still teased her by calling her "baby," but Margaret laughed. "All right, Daddy," she said. "I promise."

In September Margaret enrolled as a freshman at George Washington University. In her junior year her father was elected Vice President, but the Trumans continued to occupy the same five-room apartment. The Vice President's daughter rode the bus back and forth to classes and was also busy with voice lessons and dates and sorority activities.

Then suddenly, "everything happened"—to use Margaret's own expression. In April, 1945, Harry S. Truman became President, and a few weeks later his family moved into the White House. His only child—"the apple of his eye," he always said—was a pretty girl, with pale gold hair and a ready smile. She had been popular in college, but now she was overwhelmed with invitations. She was invited to dinners, teas, and dances. She met famous movie stars and danced with foreign diplomats. She talked with such world leaders as Winston Churchill and General George Marshall. The French general, Charles de Gaulle, gave her a wrist watch studded with diamonds. Other gifts came pouring in.

"I cannot deny that all the attention was flattering," she said. "It is tremendously exciting being the daughter of a president."

It was a heady experience for a girl of twenty-one, but her parents had faith in her. They felt sure that she would not be spoiled. "I'm not worried about Margaret," Bess Truman, her mother, told a friend. "She'll keep her feet on the ground."

Margaret proved her mother right. In some ways her life went on much as it had before. She attended classes at the university, only now she rode in a White House car and a Secret Service agent went with her. After school she saw the same friends who had liked to gather at the Truman apartment when her father was a Senator. Often after a party they came home with her and raided the family icebox on the third floor. These spur-of-the-moment gatherings were like the informal get-togethers she had enjoyed in Independence.

There were many reminders of home in her private suite on the second floor. The grand piano in her sitting room was the one that her father had given her the Christmas she was eight years old. In her bedroom, her bed was piled high with dolls and stuffed animals, including a very Republican-looking elephant and a very Democratic-looking donkey.

Margaret had long been a movie fan, and she was delighted when she visited the private movie theater in the west wing. When she was told that she could see any film she wished, she started to make a list. Some of her old favorites she saw again and again. The motion picture operator may have grown tired of showing *The Scarlet Pimpernel,* but Margaret was still enthusiastic after the sixteenth time.

The White House was an interesting place to live, and Margaret had a big bump of curiosity. She liked to think about all of the other people who had been there, from the beginning. She was amused when she heard the old rumor that it was haunted. Some of the servants said that Abraham Lincoln's ghost came back late at night. Margaret did not really believe this, but she and two chums decided that it would be a lark to sleep in the Lincoln bed. The bed was nine feet long, easily big enough to hold the three of them.

When Harry Truman learned of the plan, he considered having a member of the White House staff dress up as Lincoln and pretend to be a ghost. Then he decided that the girls might be really frightened and gave up the idea.

Meanwhile Margaret and her friends were finding their bed very uncomfortable. Mr. Lincoln's mattress was full of lumps, and they decided to sleep on the floor. They talked and giggled most of the night.

Much as Margaret liked her new life, there were disadvantages. No longer could she and Jane Lingo, her best friend, saunter up and down the avenue window-shopping or stop in somewhere for a dish of ice cream. Someone was always sure to recognize the President's daughter. People she did not know came up and shook her hand. Strangers stared at her in restaurants. Margaret took this good-naturedly.

"I've been a tourist so much," she said, "that I'm not above rubbernecking myself."

On her first visit home to Independence, Missouri, she felt a little self-conscious. Because she did not want to seem to boast, she was careful not to mention the White House. Once, when she wanted to tell her old friends about something that had happened there, she stopped in confusion. "You know," she said, "that house on Pennsylvania Avenue where Mother and Dad and I moved in last spring."

Another day at a luncheon, she met a girl who was visiting in town. The stranger was so awed, when she found herself sitting next to the President's daughter, that she could not think of anything to say.

"Please," Margaret finally burst out, "please don't be so impressed with me! I haven't done anything."

Back in Washington she continued her dizzy whirl—but never at the expense of her studies. She was a good student and was graduated near the top of her class, in June, 1946. President Truman delivered the commencement address. It was a proud moment for him when, at the request of the president of the university, he handed his daughter her diploma. She was now an A.B.—a Bachelor of Arts. A few minutes later her father was awarded the honorary degree of Doctor of Laws.

After it was all over, he started to tease her. It had taken her four years to get a degree, he insisted. It had taken him four minutes.

Margaret laughed happily. She had kept her promise. She had graduated, and now she could spend all of her time on her music. That fall she left for New York, determined to work hard and make her parents proud of her. For several months she concentrated on her singing lessons, and the following March she made her debut as a soloist with the Detroit Symphony Orchestra. Later in the same year she sang in the Hollywood Bowl and toured the South and the Southwest. She was starting the career of which she had dreamed since she was a little girl.

In 1948 she interrupted a series of concerts to help her father on a campaign tour that kept them traveling for weeks and took them through many states. In November he was elected President in his own right, and he and his family returned to Washington.

But not to stay at 1600 Pennsylvania Avenue! The mansion where thirty-one presidents had lived was no longer safe. Nearly every one of their families had made changes and repairs, and some of the remodeling had been hasty and careless. Supporting walls had been weakened when doors were cut or plumbing and heating pipes installed. The roof had been raised and the old wooden beams replaced by steel girders which were too heavy for the wooden floor just below.

Now, after nearly a century and a half, the old building could take no more abuse. It shook to the rumble of passing streetcars. Floors sagged. The heavy crystal chandelier in the East Room made strange tinkling sounds if too many people moved about in the room overhead. One day the President had gone into his daughter's sitting room and discovered that the leg of her grand piano had made a hole in the floor. The entire floor was so weak that it looked as if it might collapse into the family dining room just below.

During the next sixteen months, while the Trumans lived in Blair House down the street, a new White House was built inside the walls of the old one. When Margaret saw it again in April, 1952, it was a completely modern mansion. On the outside, the main part of the building looked much the same as it had in Andrew Jackson's time, after the north and south porticos were added. But could General Jackson or our earlier presidents have attended the reception that President and Mrs. Truman were giving that afternoon, they would have had many surprises. Besides the fifty-four rooms set aside for public entertaining and family use, there were two floors of storage and utility rooms—all underground. What had once been the kitchen, with open fireplaces, was a conference and broadcasting room. George Washington, who had approved the original plan, would have been puzzled by the air conditioning system, the busy telephone switchboard, and much of the other modern equipment.

Yet, in spite of all of the changes, it was the same White House. Through the years it had come to mean more than just the mansion where the President lived. It was a home in which millions of American people felt they had a share. Like the flag, it was a symbol. It stood for their hopes and dreams.

20 ❧ The Young Eisenhowers and the "Children" Who Came Back

Dwight David Eisenhower 2d, aged five, had never seen so many rooms. He glanced around the entrance hall of the White House and walked up the impressive stairway to the second floor where his grandparents had their private suite. On the third floor he was shown the nursery where he and his sisters, Barbara Anne and baby Susan, were to stay. David turned a puzzled face up to his grandmother.

"Mimi," he asked, "why do you live in such a big house?"

Mamie Eisenhower squeezed his hand. "It isn't my house, David. It belongs to Uncle Sam," she said.

"Mimi" was a pet name for the new First Lady, and he called the President "Ike." General Eisenhower had suggested it, when David was just a baby and found "grandfather" a hard word to pronounce. One day when the general was making a speech, David was in the audience. A man who had noticed a family resemblance came up to him afterwards.

"What is your name?" he asked.

"Dwight David Eisenhower."

"Then who is that up there?" The man pointed to the platform.

"Oh," said the little boy, "that's Ike."

David was not the first person who had used this nickname. "General Ike," as his soldiers called him, had become a popular hero during World War II. He was also a hero to his grandchildren. David confided to his mother that he had three favorite people. Ike came first, and then Mimi. His third choice was Santa Claus.

It was almost like paying a visit to Santa Claus to visit at the White House, with its private swimming pool and projection room for showing movies. In the garden a swing hung invitingly from the branch of a tall Norwegian maple. There were acres of lawn where Skunky, a small black

Scotty, could pretend to chase rabbits and David could chase Skunky.

A favorite place to play was Mimi's room, with an over-sized bed on which to bounce. The grandchildren frequently joined her while she had her breakfast tray. Barbara Anne usually brought some of her dolls along. Susie had her blocks. David raced his new fire engine across the carpet or flew his model planes. Sometimes he pretended to be a plane, spreading his make-believe wings and flying around the room.

"Look at it zoom!" he shouted. "Watch me, Mimi."

Mimi chuckled fondly. She liked to start her busy day by playing with the children or by telling them a story. To her friends she cheerfully admitted that she had what she called "grandmother's disease."

On one occasion the wife of the President of Turkey called on Mrs. Eisenhower. Neither could speak the other's language, but when the visiting First Lady brought out a picture of her grandchildren, Mimi smiled in appreciation. She also had a picture to show—one of David, Barbara Anne, and Susie. The caller admired them in Turkish, but her hostess understood exactly what she meant. There was nothing Mamie Eisenhower liked better than to talk about her grandchildren, or to watch them enjoying themselves at the White House.

On Easter Monday their pleasure was shared by thousands of others. The custom of egg rolling had been given up after the United States entered World War II. Now, fourteen years later, President and Mrs. Eisenhower invited the boys and girls of Washington to come to the south grounds, just as many of their parents and grandparents had come before them. John, the young Eisenhowers' dad, had been one of the egg rollers on the lawn the year that he was five. Much had happened since then. At thirty-one, he was a major fighting in another war on the other side of the world. After a brief visit in January, 1953, when President Eisenhower was inaugurated, John had returned to his unit in Korea.

"I missed him terribly," said Barbara, his charming young wife, "and so did the children."

They seemed to miss him all the more after they returned to the town in New York state where they were living at that time. One night when David was saying his prayers, his mother heard him add, "Please bring Daddy home, so we can be a whole family again."

His prayer was answered. By the next September, Major John Eisenhower returned to the United States. During the next year and a half he and his family lived near several different army posts where he was on duty. Then he was assigned to Fort Belvoir in Alexandria, Virginia, across the river from Washington. Just before Christmas, 1955, a new baby, Mary Jean, was born.

In Alexandria, David, Anne, and Susie attended school and lived in much the same way as did the sons and daughters of other young army officers. There was one difference —the Eisenhowers had a second home in the White House. They spent many week ends, as well as longer vacations, with Ike and Mimi. Ike, whose favorite game was golf, had given David a miniature set of golf clubs, and they sometimes practiced their strokes in the rose garden. Barbara

Anne, who was taking ballet lessons, liked to show her grandfather the latest step that she had learned. Susan thought it a treat to visit his office in the west wing and use a typewriter belonging to one of the secretaries. Mary Jean climbed into his lap and drew pictures for him.

Although Mary Jean was too young to share in all of the good times, David took her for rides in his small electric car around the White House drive. She went in swimming but stayed in the shallow end of the pool and played with a big yellow rubber duck. The others were learning to dive into deep water. They jumped in, feet first, and swam out forty-five feet into the pool. They practiced until they could swim a hundred yards, half of that distance on their backs. The year that David was ten, Barbara eight, and Susan six, they passed their Intermediate Class swimming tests and were awarded American Red Cross certificates and buttons.

One of their most interesting adventures was their first ride in the helicopter parked on the lawn. Up, up, they went, feeling much the way they did when they rode in an elevator. They looked down on the White House roof and then were whisked away to the Eisenhower farm near Gettysburg, Pennsylvania.

With four children, there were many birthday celebrations, but the year that David had a Wild West party, his sisters were not invited. When his guests, all boys, gathered around the table, they saw a procession of toy cowboys astride miniature ponies galloping down the middle to form a centerpiece. At each end of the table there was a toy corral, and the birthday cake also resembled a corral. The decorations were make believe, but the tall young man who stood at the head of the table, strumming a guitar, was real. The children stared when they saw his guns, and the chaps and cowboy boots that he was wearing. He grinned at them and began to sing:

"Whoop-pee ti yi yo, git along little dogies. . . ."

David and his friends had seen Roy Rogers, "the king of the cowboys," in the movies, but never had they expected to meet him in person. He sang their favorite cowboy songs and told them story after story of Trigger, his famous horse.

As David grew older he cared a little less about cowboys and much more about golf and baseball. The year that he was eleven, he attended his first big league baseball game. With two of his fifth-grade friends, he arrived at the ball park early, and they lunched on hot dogs and ice cream. This was the first game of the season for the Washington Senators, and the stadium was crowded. The President had been asked to toss the first ball, and a special glove had been made for him. But he was out of town, and the honor fell to his grandson.

"Standing in a flag-bedecked box," one newspaper reported, "David took a practice toss at the infield. The glove was given to him as a gift."

Because David was the oldest, more people knew about him, but his three pretty sisters shared equally in their grandparents' affection. The President was especially interested in their studies.

"I encourage good grades in my grandchildren in this way," he said. "I give them two bucks for each A, nothing for a B plus; and if they get below a B, they have to give me a buck."

He admitted that they had collected a good many dollars from him, but he did not seem to mind.

Like their brother David, Barbara Anne, Susan and little Mary Jean all felt very much at home in the White House. They may have been surprised to learn how many other boys and girls had once lived there. On April 30, 1959, eight sons and daughters of former presidents gathered in Washington for a reunion. They were grown up now, but for that one day they all felt young again. They joked and called one another "children" and "fellow descendants" and "fellow members of the 1600 Pennsylvania Avenue gang."

On the way to a tea at the White House, Eleanor Wilson McAdoo passed along some of the same wide tree-lined avenues that she and Margaret Wilson had traveled on that hilarious day when they had pretended to be sightseers on a rubberneck wagon. Marion Cleveland Amen, glancing up at the white pillars, was reminded of the toy White House that she and her sisters had played with when they were small.

Mrs. Eisenhower was waiting on the steps of the north portico to welcome her visitors. "Come in and join me," she said. "There have been many changes since you were here."

Her guests included not only sons and daughters but a host of grandchildren and great-grandchildren down to the sixth generation. Two descendants of Nelly Custis came to see the house that George Washington had planned. The great-great-great-great-great-great-granddaughter of John and Abigail Adams stood beside her. Four descendants of Thomas Jefferson looked across the rolling lawn toward the white marble memorial erected in his memory. Descendants of several other presidents followed Mrs. Eisenhower as she showed her guests through the remodeled mansion.

The sons and daughters who had lived there found the second floor, with its new decorations, much lighter and more cheerful than they remembered it. The musty attic where Charles Taft had liked to roughhouse with Quentin Roosevelt had been turned into suites of attractive rooms. Quentin's sister, Alice Roosevelt Longworth, could recall how she and the other children of Theodore Roosevelt used to slide down the stairs on a large tray from the pantry. James Roosevelt was thinking of the time during World War II when he had served as an aide to his father, Franklin D. Roosevelt.

John Coolidge, with his two pretty daughters, Cynthia and Lydia, paused before the Howard Chandler Christy portrait of his mother. The picture of Mrs. Calvin Coolidge, with her white collie beside her, caught the special warmth that had made her so many friends. Peggy Ann Hoover Brigham saw the fireplace where Santa Claus had miraculously appeared one Christmas morning when she was visiting her grandfather, Herbert Hoover. Helen Taft Manning remembered how she and her friends had played "Sardines" in the big rooms.

"What fun it was to live in the White House in our day!" she said.

For each of her "fellow children" the house held glowing memories. Major John Eisenhower was storing up memories for the future. "In years to come," he said, with a glance toward his wife, "Barbara and I will look back on the White House with a mixture of affection and awe."

David, Barbara Anne, Susan, and Mary Jean, although they were not there, knew about this unusual tea party. Perhaps some day another reunion would be held, and they could be present. For President Eisenhower's grandchildren were also to join that group of former children who had once lived at 1600 Pennsylvania Avenue. They, too, would doubtless look back on the days when they had romped on the wide lawns with the same awe and affection of which their father spoke.

ࢥ What Happened Later

You have been reading about a number of the younger residents and visitors to the White House. The following brief paragraphs tell a little of what happened to some of them when they grew older.

GEORGE WASHINGTON'S FAMILY: Nelly Custis married Lawrence Lewis, General Washington's favorite nephew, and lived for many years at Woodlawn, an estate not far from Mt. Vernon. Her brother, George Washington Parke Custis, grew up to be a gentleman as dignified as his name. He wrote a book, *Recollections of Washington,* and built a mansion called Arlington across the river from the capital. His son-in-law, Robert E. Lee, the great Confederate general, lived in the same mansion. Now a part of Arlington National Cemetery, this house is open to the public.

JOHN ADAMS' GRANDCHILDREN: Susanna Adams grew up in Quincy, Massachusetts, where her grandparents lived after they left the White House. The ex-President was very proud of her. She developed such a good handwriting that she copied some of his important papers, and on one occasion he gave her a pearl ring to show his gratitude. She always treasured it, especially the words engraved inside the band: *This is a reward for your industry.*

Susanna was not only industrious but witty and charming. After her marriage to a Lieutenant Clark, she returned to

[178]

Washington, where she was very popular. With her own little Susan she often visited the White House while her uncle, John Quincy Adams, lived there. Susanna's cousin, Johnny Smith, who as a small boy had played horse with a dignified Vice President, became a lawyer.

THOMAS JEFFERSON'S GRANDCHILDREN: Our third President was a very generous man, but he died a poor one. He left many debts which his grandson, Thomas Jefferson Randolph, undertook to pay. "Jeff," as his family called him, edited his grandfather's letters for publication, was a member of the Virginia Legislature for many years, and served as a Visitor at the University of Virginia, the college founded by Thomas Jefferson.

Ellen, one of the little Randolph girls who visited at the White House, grew up to marry Thomas Coolidge, and her sister Virginia married Nicholas Trist. Both of their husbands became well-known diplomats. Their cousin, Francis Eppes, together with several members of the Randolph family, settled in western Florida when it was still a wilderness. Monticello, the beautiful home which Thomas Jefferson designed and built, and where he spent his last years surrounded by his grandchildren, is now visited by hundreds of tourists every month.

DOLLEY MADISON'S RELATIVES: "Queen Dolley" had been away from Washington for twenty years when she returned there to live. James Madison had died; and the Cutts children, whom she had loved so dearly, were all grown. But now there was a host of her grandnephews and grandnieces who adored her. Dolley was very poor because of the extravagance of her son, Payne Todd, who had piled up huge debts that his mother had to pay. Finally Congress voted to offer her $20,000 for the remaining papers and letters of her late husband. James Madison Cutts, Jr.—her "little Madison," Dolley called him—was in the Senate with his father, who sent him on ahead to tell his aunt.

"Well do I remember running from the Senate Chambers the moment the Senate passed the bill," he recalled years later. "I arrived out of breath, the first to bring her the glad news which made us all happy for her dear sake."

JAMES MONROE'S YOUNGER DAUGHTER: Maria, the first White House bride, lived with her husband, Samuel Gouverneur, in New York for many years. She was fond of books, occasionally wrote verses, and was happy in the companionship of her three children and later her grandchildren. She frequently visited Washington, and in her later years spent part of each year at Oak Hill, her father's old home in Virginia. This house is now open to the public. One of her descendants, Rose Governeur Hoes, assembled the dresses of most of our first ladies, and planned the exhibit that may still be seen in the Smithsonian Institution.

JOHN QUINCY ADAMS' FAMILY: A few years after John Quincy finished his one term as President, he was elected to Congress and went back to Washington to live. Mary Louisa, the little granddaughter born in the White House, grew up in his home after her own father died. John Quincy Adams adored her and, as he had hoped, taught her to read at a very early age. As a young woman, she married her cousin, William Charles Johnson, and went to live in Utica, New York.

Charles Francis Adams, the youngest son, who was eighteen when his father was inaugurated, became famous as an author and a diplomat. He represented the United States in England (1861–1868) during one of the most difficult periods in our history.

ANDREW JACKSON'S FAMILY: The Donelson children lived abroad for several years. Their father was a diplomat, and by the time he returned to the United States Mary Emily (who wrote the story of "Christmas With Old Hickory") was grown up. She married the Honorable John. A. Wilcox, a member of Congress, but they went south to live when the War Between the States broke out. The war swept away their fortune, and after her husband's death Mary Emily brought her two small children to Washington. She became a translator in the post office department and held other government positions. Many times she walked past the Treasury Building where one of her golden curls—clipped from her head by a doting uncle years before—lay preserved in the cornerstone.

The three boys who were a part of President Jackson's household served as soldiers in the Confederate armies, and one of them, John Donelson, was killed in battle. Little Rachel Jackson grew up to marry Dr. John Lawrence of Nashville, and lived not far from The Hermitage, the handsome house built by her grandfather. She was a charter member of the Ladies' Hermitage Association, which restored the house so that the American people might see it as it had looked when General Jackson lived there.

JOHN TYLER'S SONS: A year before John Tyler left the White House, his eldest son, Robert, moved with his wife, Priscilla, and little daughter, Mary Fairlee, to Philadelphia. Here Robert became a successful lawyer and political leader. At the outbreak of the War Between the States, because he remained loyal to the South, he and his family were forced to flee to his native Virginia. After the war he moved to Montgomery, Alabama, where again he became a leader and helped his adopted state through the difficult period of reconstruction. A younger brother, Tazewell Tyler, studied medicine and joined the medical corps of the Confederate army.

ABRAHAM LINCOLN'S SONS: After Abraham Lincoln was shot, his son, Tad, seemed to change overnight from an irresponsible youngster into a serious-minded youth. He studied hard and was his mother's greatest comfort. The two of them lived in Chicago and then went abroad for a year. He studied with a tutor and, according to Noah Brooks, he "made such progress that his friends entertained for him the brightest hopes." But Tad's work was done. He died shortly after his return to Chicago, at the age of eighteen. Julia Taft, who at sixteen knew Tad and Willie and later told their story, married a Congregational minister and lived in New England.

Of the Lincoln sons, only Robert lived to manhood. He became a successful lawyer and businessman, served in the cabinets of Presidents James A. Garfield and Chester A. Arthur, and was appointed by President Benjamin Harrison to represent the United States in Great Britain.

ANDREW JOHNSON'S HOUSEHOLD: Andrew Johnson, Jr., (who was called Frank in the family) published a newspaper, the Greenville *Intelligencer,* in his home town in Tennessee, when he was only twenty-one years old. He died a few years later, at the start of a promising career. Andrew Johnson Patterson, the oldest grandson who lived in the White House as a boy, grew up to serve in the Tennessee legislature and as United States consul to British Guiana.

WHAT HAPPENED LATER

The Andrew Johnson home in Greenville, in which Andrew Johnson Patterson and his family continued to live for many years, has now been restored and is open to the public.

GENERAL GRANT'S FAMILY: The lovely Nellie Grant was married in the White House at eighteen and went to live in England. Her younger brother, Jesse, entered Cornell College at sixteen. Many years later, in 1921, an interesting reunion took place in Washington. Jesse Grant and twenty-four other members of the K.F.R. (the secret society which had started with six boys) came together to celebrate their fifty years of friendship. A number of them had served in the Army and Navy during World War I. Others had become successful doctors, lawyers, clergymen, writers, diplomats, and businessmen.

The two older Grant sons both had interesting careers. Ulysses, Jr., became a lawyer, Fred a colonel in the Army. After Fred's marriage in 1875, he brought his bride to the White House, where their daughter Julia was born. She grew up to marry a Russian nobleman, Prince Cantacuzene, lived through the Russian Revolution, and later returned to Washington. She wrote several books about her experiences.

RUTHERFORD B. HAYES' FAMILY: Webb C. Hayes, who as a young man in the White House sometimes had to sleep on a billiard table because his mother had so many guests, served as a colonel in the Spanish-American War. He was awarded the Congressional Medal of Honor for his bravery, and later served in World War I. In the meantime, he had organized a small business that became a big one—the Union Carbide Corporation. For many years, Webb lived at Spiegel Grove, the wooded family estate near Fremont,

Ohio. Later, he and his brothers and sister gave it to the state to be preserved as a memorial to their father, and Webb donated the money to build the Rutherford B. Hayes Library. This library houses a large collection of books, papers, and other exhibits pertaining to the Hayes family and their times.

The younger brother, Scott, became a successful business-man in New York City, where he was connected with firms manufacturing railroad equipment. His sister Fanny married Ensign Harry Eaton Smith of the United States Navy, later an instructor at the Naval Academy in Annapolis, Maryland. Her last years were spent in New England, where she lived to be eighty-two.

JAMES GARFIELD'S FAMILY: The four Garfield sons became men of influence. Each of them attended Williams College, of which Harry Garfield later became president. During World War II he served as United States Fuel Administrator, and later he was awarded the Distinguished Service Medal. James Garfield became a lawyer, and was Secretary of the Interior in Theodore Roosevelt's cabinet. Irvin, who had ridden a high-wheeled bicycle down the grand staircase at the White House, grew up to be a successful lawyer in Boston. Abram, the boy who liked to draw, became a well-known architect, and served as president of the Cleveland City Plan Commission. Mollie, the only daughter, married her father's secretary, Stanley Brown, who later became an investment banker. Her last years were spent in New York and Pasadena, California.

CHESTER A. ARTHUR'S FAMILY: After leaving the White House, Nell Arthur attended a boarding school in Farmington, Connecticut, where Fanny Hayes and Mollie Garfield, daughters of two former presidents, were students at the same time. After her marriage to Charles Pinkerton, she continued to live in New York City. Her brother Alan traveled widely, was interested in art, and took part in polo games and other sports. His last years were spent in Colorado Springs, Colorado.

BENJAMIN HARRISON'S GRANDCHILDREN: Benjamin Harrison McKee (whom the newspapers once called "Baby Mc-Kee,") became a successful banker. For several years before his retirement he was connected with the Paris office of the National City Bank of New York. He was living in Nice, France, at the time of his death in 1958. Mary McKee Reisinger, his cousin, lived in New York after her marriage. Another granddaughter, Marthena Harrison Williams, served in the Veterans' Bureau during World War II. She still lives in Washington not far from the White House where she played as a little girl.

GROVER CLEVELAND'S FAMILY: After the Clevelands went to Princeton, New Jersey, to live, two sons, Francis and Richard, were added to the family. Ruth, the eldest child, died when she was only twelve. Esther, who was born in the White House, grew up and did war work in Europe during World War I. Her marriage to an English officer, Captain William Bosanquet, took place in Westminster Abbey, and they now live in Yorkshire, England. Marion, the youngest of the three sisters, married John Amen, a New York attorney. She now devotes most of her time to the Girl Scouts, serving in the public relations department of the New York headquarters. At a luncheon reunion of presidents' sons and daughters held in Washington in the spring of 1959, Richard Cleveland, a Baltimore lawyer, humorously remarked, "For a person who was never in the White House until Mrs. Coolidge was kind enough to invite me to tea some years ago, it is surprising how many people remember seeing me play around the grounds."

THEODORE ROOSEVELT'S CHILDREN: Quentin Roosevelt crowded much adventure and fun and bravery into his short life. As a flier in World War I, he was barely twenty-one when his plane was shot down over enemy lines. His three brothers served as officers in the same war, and again in World War II. All four were decorated for bravery. They also won success in civilian life. Theodore, Jr., was Assistant Secretary of the Navy, Governor of Puerto Rico, and Governor General of the Philippines. Kermit's work as secretary of the American Ship and Commerce Corporation took him all over the world. Archibald (known as Archie during his White House days) became an investment banker.

Theodore Roosevelt's younger daughter, Ethel Roosevelt Darby, married a Long Island physician and lives near the old family home at Oyster Bay. The older daughter, once known as Princess Alice, married Nicholas Longworth, who was to become the Speaker of the House of Representatives. She still lives in Washington, D.C.

WILLIAM HOWARD TAFT'S FAMILY: After leaving the White House, Helen Taft finished her studies at Bryn Mawr College, where she was appointed dean of the college at the age of twenty-five. Later she was acting president, and then head of the department of history. She married Frederick Manning, also a professor of history.

Her younger brother, Charles, after serving as a lieutenant in World War I, returned to Yale to finish his college course and to graduate from the Yale Law School.

In Cincinnati, where he practiced law, he was one of the founders of a successful city manager system of government, and later became mayor. Meanwhile during World War II he had served as director of the Office of Maritime Economic Affairs. In 1946 he became president of the Federal Council of Churches.

The older brother, Robert Taft, who was nicknamed "Mr. Republican," was a leader in the United States Senate for a number of years. After his death, the impressive Taft Tower was erected on the Capitol grounds in his memory.

WOODROW WILSON'S FAMILY: Eleanor, the youngest daughter, who married William Gibbs McAdoo, Secretary of the Treasury, while she was a girl in the White House, later went to live in California. She wrote an interesting book called *The Woodrow Wilsons.* Margaret, the oldest of the three Wilson girls, spent her last years in India, where she died in 1944. Jessie, the wife of Francis B. Sayre, a professor at Harvard, continued to be interested in welfare movements until her death in 1933. Her eldest child, Francis B. Sayre, Jr., who had been born in the White House, grew up to become a Protestant Episcopalian clergyman, and at the age of thirty-six was appointed Dean of the National Cathedral in Washington. One of the tasks that lay ahead of him was to raise funds to complete the beautiful Gothic edifice that has been called "the Westminster Abbey of America."

CALVIN COOLIDGE'S SONS: Many older people will always think of Calvin, Jr., as a boy, because he died when he was only sixteen. Several years later, when ex-President Coolidge wrote his *Autobiography,* he sent a copy of the book to another father who had lost a child. *To my friend,* read the inscription on the flyleaf, *in recollection of his son and my son, who, by the grace of God, have the privilege of being boys throughout eternity.*

John Coolidge, the older brother, graduated from Amherst College and became a successful businessman in Connecticut. After his retirement, he plans to spend more time in Plymouth, Vermont, where his father was born, and to reopen an old cheese factory in which his grandfather had been one of the first shareholders.

HERBERT HOOVER'S GRANDCHILDREN: Peggy Ann Hoover, after her graduation from Wellesley College, worked for the National Polio Foundation at the Children's Hospital in Boston. She married Richard Tatem Brigham, a young Boston businessman. Her younger sister, Joan, is now Mrs. William Leland Vowles, and lives in California. Herbert Hoover 3d, who had been called Peter as a child, also lives in California. Like his grandfather and his father, he became an engineer.

FRANKLIN D. ROOSEVELT'S GRANDCHILDREN: Anna Eleanor Dall, perhaps the best known among the many grandchildren during the time that her grandfather was president, married Van H. Seagraves of Oregon. For several years the young couple lived in Paris where he was an economist employed by the Mutual Security Agency. In 1959, the former "Sistie" was living in Lake Placid, New York, with her husband and their three small children. Her brother, Curtis, once called "Buzzie," is now a vice president of the New School for Social Research in New York City. Diana Hopkins, who for five years had enjoyed all the privileges of a grandchild in the Roosevelt household, attended Bryn Mawr College. She also studied in Switzerland and at the

School of Foreign Service at Georgetown University. In 1953 she became Mrs. Allin Preston Baxter.

HARRY S. TRUMAN'S DAUGHTER: Margaret Truman's book, *Souvenir,* told of her experiences in the White House and of her career as a singer. In 1956 she married Clifton Daniel, a member of the staff of the *New York Times* and a former foreign correspondent for that paper. They have two sons, Clifton Truman and William Wallace. Mrs. Daniel continued to make occasional television and stage appearances after her marriage.

ABOUT THE AUTHOR

Frances Cavanah finds it hard to decide which she enjoys more—writing or editing books for young people. A native Hoosier, she was graduated from DePauw University, and then joined the staff of the old *Child Life*. One of her duties as associate editor was to read thousands of letters that poured in from youthful subscribers, and the insight she gained into their thinking proved invaluable. Later, she was biography editor of a young people's encyclopedia, and then director of *Real People,* a series of biographies widely used in schools. She has combined her talents as an editor and as a writer in several anthologies. *They Lived in the White House,* though not strictly an anthology, includes several firsthand accounts by younger members of our presidential households, thus sharpening the sense of immediacy that Miss Cavanah strives for in all of her books.

Miss Cavanah's books include *Two Loves for Jenny Lind,* the story, newly told, of the beloved singer's American tour and romance; *Holiday Round Up,* in collaboration with Lucile Pannell; and *We Came to America,* based on first-person accounts of people from other lands. Two of her titles have been made into talking books, and several have been transcribed into Braille and translated into other languages. Miss Cavanah now makes her home in Washington and much of her research is done at the Library of Congress. She feels that to succeed in pleasing children is a reward in itself, inasmuch as there is no audience in the world more appreciative.